IT BEGAN
WITH A
PROMISE

It Began with a Promise

Demystifying Biblical Narratives for Teachers

Richard Olson

NOVALIS

© 2013 Novalis Publishing Inc.

Cover: Martin Gould
Cover photo by Splitcast / iStockphoto
Layout: Audrey Wells

Published by Novalis

Publishing Office
10 Lower Spadina Avenue, Suite 400
Toronto, Ontario, Canada
M5V 2Z2

Head Office
4475 Frontenac Street
Montréal, Québec, Canada
H2H 2S2

www.novalis.ca

Library and Archives Canada Cataloguing in Publication

Olson, Richard, 1963-
     It began with a promise : demystifying biblical narratives for teachers /
Richard Olson.

ISBN 978-2-89646-532-3

     1. Bible--Study and teaching. I. Title.

BS600.3.O47 2013   220.071   C2013-901703-8

Printed in Canada.

We acknowledge the financial support of the Government of Canada through the Canada Book Fund for business development activities.

5 4 3 2 1   17 16 15 14 13

For

Andrea,
with whom I share a promise:
in her love and care
all things seem possible
&
for Walt and Jack,
the very flesh of the promise
in whom your mother and father delight

Acknowledgements

This work would not have been possible without the dedication of faith-filled teachers who nurtured within me a deep appreciation for God's Word revealed. I work from a deep debt of gratitude for my first scripture teacher on the prairies, Gisele Bauche, and for my mentor, Father Walter Wadey (d. 1995). Additionally, I extend thanks to Tim Hegedus and the Waterloo Lutheran Seminary at Wilfrid Laurier University, who encouraged the earliest version of this manuscript with their commitment to contextual theology and ecumenical study. Finally, this resource would never have been made available to teachers without the support of Novalis Publishing. In particular, I would like to express my thanks to Joseph Sinasac, Grace Deutsch, Glenn Byer, Don Beyers, and Anne Louise Mahoney.

Contents

Introduction

A few years ago, in a Grade 10 religion class, I referred to the story of Saul on the road to Damascus. The response? Blank stares and puzzled frowns. Virtually no one in the group knew this key story from the Acts of the Apostles (9:1-9). A few months later, I was sharing this experience with a group of adult religious educators. I told them I could no longer assume that students in today's Catholic high schools were familiar with core New Testament stories. One young teacher sheepishly raised her hand and asked, "What *is* the story about the road to Damascus?"

This led me to wonder whether there was a connection between the biblical illiteracy of the teacher and that of the teen. As a condition of employment, most Ontario Catholic school boards require teachers to complete Religious Education (RE) Part 1; this and other additional qualification courses for teachers have a significant scripture component. Still, many teachers and students display biblical illiteracy. Was the first group simply influencing the second? Or were there other, less apparent connections – such as the influence of the dominant secular, diverse and post-Christian culture? When both teens and adults don't know the core biblical stories, how does this compromise their understanding of the gospel of Jesus and limit how well they can live it?

My experience in teaching biblical narrative has led me to draw the following six conclusions.

1. **Many religious educators (and adult Christians generally) are scripturally illiterate, yet spiritually starving.**

While many religious educators do not know the Bible, they are hungry to learn more when given the opportunity. Others who are called upon to teach religious education do not have sufficient experience with biblical spirituality. In either case, biblical literacy is needed for the success of the educator and learner alike.

2. **Biblical illiteracy compromises the proclamation of the gospel.**

Fuzzy thinking or confusion about the Bible's story leads to ineffective catechesis (instruction in the faith) and ineffective evangelization (proclamation of the faith). It is also more likely to lead to a secularization of the Bible stories presented in the classroom.[1] For example, a religious education teacher who is not familiar with the core biblical themes might present a Bible story in a way that reflects secular rather than Christian values. The story of David and Goliath then becomes a lesson in the perseverance and courage of the underdog instead of a story about a young man anointed with the charism of God. When biblical narratives are secularized, the agency (action) of God is removed.

3. **Learners' faith development is arrested when they lack knowledge of the Bible, its core stories and key themes.**

If learners do not explore the Bible in a systematic and structured way, the impetus to grow in their faith or do any significant thinking and praying about their journey of faith may be minimized.

James Fowler outlines six stages of faith that are part of the psychology of human development.

- Stage 1: Intuitive-Projective: Occurs between the ages of three and seven. This is the stage where the child absorbs cultural taboos and accepts unconditionally the parent's view of the world, including religious views.

- Stage 2: Mythic-Literal. A literal interpretation of biblical events, for example, is prominent as the imagination runs freely and every action is characterized as either right or wrong.

- Stage 3: Synthetic-Conventional. Faith has become an important part of how the individual orders his or her world; conformity to the larger social group is evident.

- Stage 4: Individuative-Reflective. Characterized by a deep personal questioning of one's beliefs and some detachment from a previously defining group. One is usually well into adulthood before entering this stage.

- Stage 5: Conjunctive. A person discovers a deep sense of mystery with the attendant acknowledgement of paradox and transcendence.

- Stage 6: Universalizing. The individual encounters a transcendent moral and religious sense of being that leads to activism or an enhanced sense of service to the human community.

James Fowler's work has made a significant contribution to religious education, enriching our understanding of the journey of faith through stages of natural development.[2]

Leading religious educator Gabriel Moran collapses Fowler's six stages to three movements in religious education: Simply Religious, Christian Education, and Religiously Christian.[3] Moran explains,

With the advent of self-reflective consciousness, childhood's naiveté is forever lost. Adolescence pushes aside the magical, superstitious, and religious in favour of calculative and instrumental rationality. The adolescent is looking for measurable things and reasonable explanations. Adulthood is the discovery that childhood was not all in error and that rational control needs a religious context of mystery and wonder.[4]

He names the forms that education takes – family, work, school and leisure – and then connects them to the process of religious education and the journey of faith. In this way, family becomes *community*, work becomes *vocation*, school becomes *vision*, and leisure becomes *contemplation*.

Moran contends that one understanding of Religious Education might be that which "affirms the family while at the same time reminding the family that it is not the final community."[5] Helping adults make the connection between their own family dynamics and those embedded in the biblical narrative increases their awareness of the sense of the larger community that is integral to the kingdom of God. Moran's approach has helped to shape my own approach in this book.

Father James T. Mulligan's extensive qualitative research on Catholic education reveals a number of factors that determine the sustainability of a Catholic/Christian publicly funded education system in the province of Ontario. In an increasingly secular, pluralistic and multi-faith society, the "on-going faith formation of the Catholic teacher is the number one priority in terms of ensuring a future for Catholic education in the province of Ontario," he says.[6] Mulligan has found that since 1985, when Premier Bill Davis extended full funding to Grades 11, 12 and 13, Catholic education has devolved into a kind of malaise of entitlement. For Catholics, full funding has meant increased responsibility and accountability to demonstrate that their education system is distinct from other publicly funded systems in the province. Mulligan asserts repeatedly that teachers in Catholic schools must be animated by the Catholic/Christian story. Ignorance leads to ambivalence, in his view; the end result could be the loss of public funding for faith education of any kind in Ontario.

Mulligan's work is informative and enlightening, yet it does not refer explicitly to biblical illiteracy. When it comes to the Catholic/Christian story, a greater knowledge of and facility with scripture is key to a deeper understanding of the Church, the sacraments and the gospel – which all religious educators need to engage in the work of catechesis or evangelization.

4. Most "how to read the Bible" books are too ambitious for today's readers.

The general approach is to use study notes for the books of the Bible in order of their appearance. Both the Biblos Project[7] and the noted American biblical scholar and theologian Walter Brueggemann instead recommend a thematic approach to the Bible that focuses on the meaning of the biblical narrative. (See #6 below.)

5. If learners cannot see the relevance of the scriptures to their lives, they will turn away.[8]

Research about adult learning, especially as it relates to religious education, reinforces this finding, but is true for learners of every age.[9] We can organize the Bible's story in a way that is accessible to the life experience of the learners.[10]

Teens and adults approach biblical narratives differently. For teens, moving from a focus on *what happens in the story* to *what the story means* is difficult. They tend to be very literal minded: for example, a teenage boy may conclude that the story of the exodus has no connection to his life because he isn't a slave living in Egypt. On the other hand, teachers make this movement quite easily. Because of their work experience with bosses and managers and principals, they have a profound understanding of Pharaoh in their lives.

6. Reluctant learners will not try to learn unless they are given manageable "chunks" in a sequence and language they understand.

Many learners and religious educators alike think that coming to a better understanding of the biblical narrative is too big a task, given their starting point. A popular and effective approach is to break down the task into manageable bits that can be tackled one at a time. For this reason, I begin with the key stories of the Old and New Testaments. Once we establish that the stories of Exodus and Resurrection are the prisms through which we view the other narratives, the themes of covenant and kingdom of God become more comprehensible.

The research findings of the Biblos Project and the work of Walter Brueggemann both support this approach. Brueggemann writes, "This thematization is our required work and our most profound hazard."[11] Given the breadth and scope of the Old Testament, for example, the themes we promote are likely to be fragmentary. We proceed anyway, in the hope and conviction that something meaningful can be expressed about our relationship *with* and understanding *of* God.

Brueggemann refers to the *primal narrative*, the *extended narrative* and the *derivative narrative* as a way of mastering the Bible's story, because "[t]he Bible is a strange book that is put together in an odd way. It seems to have no order at all but is a jumbled collection hard to penetrate."[12] I take a similar approach, calling the primal narratives of the Old and New Testament *seed stories*. The extended narratives related to covenant and kingdom of God I call *boundary markers* or *theme stories* that support the seed stories. The seed stories are the keys to understanding the Bible. With these keys, either by independent study or advanced formation, the boundary markers or theme stories can be opened up and better understood.

For whom is this book intended?

This book is for the many teachers in religious education classrooms who feel under-qualified to teach using the Bible. They may be familiar with a variety of Bible stories but they do not have a solid grasp of the architecture of the biblical narrative itself. If they can't see the big picture, they can't plumb the depths of the key themes out of which God speaks. If religious educators are not tuned to the frequency of divine revelation, then the good news that the Bible proclaims is distorted or lost. Biblical illiteracy compromises the very word of God that is being spoken from the depth of our tradition.[13]

How to Open the Bible

Why study the Bible?

If you grew up in the 1970s or have listened to classic rock radio, Jeremiah was a bullfrog. But if you become a student of the biblical narrative where God speaks words of life and transformation, Jeremiah is a prophet, someone God speaks to and, in turn, someone who speaks for God. The words of life that come from the effervescent, vivacious reality of God were delivered to Jeremiah. He found that he could not stop their flow. If he tried, his very bones would burn within him (see Jeremiah 20:9). Just as God called Jeremiah, God may be calling your students!

The Bible can be understood as the conversation that first Jews and later Christians have been carrying on with God for a long, long time. For Christians, the Bible is an unfolding or unpacking of our understanding of God that has been revealed over time. The library we call the Bible is not covered in the dust of centuries of neglect, but brimming with the living waters of God's word for the world. No one should go to the Bible lightly, for it is a living, generative word that has the power to transform lives. In a sense, this is a "buyer beware" bulletin. Wade into the turbulent, white-hot water of divine revelation that is the Christian Bible and your very life may be challenged! This can sound like bad news. Some people who are comfortable with their lives react negatively whenever someone says something like, "Read this book. It will change your life." The skeptic or the complacent person may not desire a change of life or may be very cautious of the kind of change it might entail. Change can be scary. The unknown always bustles with dragons. But there is good news, too.

The good news is that coming to a greater understanding of the biblical narrative is liberating. Literally! God's word to us over the past 30 centuries spanning the Judeo-Christian tradition has been one of joy; it has been good news! It has meant home and family. It has meant the healing of wounds. It is a promise not just of life, but of abundant life: "I come that they may have life, and have it abundantly" (John 10:10).

The Bible helps us to see how God speaks to us in a variety of ways. In these days of climate change and other dire environmental issues, Christians believe that God speaks to us from the mysterious grandeur of the cosmos, from the richly complex, diverse and delicate balance of our natural world. Christians believe that God has spoken most definitively in the person and mission of Jesus Christ. And while Catholic Christians believe that God continues to speak and act through the Church and the sacraments, the larger Christian community has always placed great emphasis in God's self-revelation through the Word – Jesus Christ. Believers who are immersed in a life of prayerful contemplation know that God's voice is heard in our dreams and in the deep longings of our hearts. Those who are dedicated to interfaith dialogue and ecumenism believe that God speaks to humanity through the diverse beauty and richness of the world's faith traditions. The Bible is not just a single book – it is a library containing a collection of many books[14] written by many authors[15] over a period of around a thousand years.

Inukshuk – Marking the way forward

Before the invention of global positioning systems (GPS) that are so portable, convenient and widely used today, the Inuit of the far north used the *inukshuk* – a figure of a human made from stones – to mark passages in remote wilderness areas. These figures reassured travellers that they were going the right way or that caches of food were nearby. In vast areas with few markers to indicate direction, inukshuk were invaluable signposts for the wayward and hungry that others had gone before them and that they would not starve or become lost on their journey.

In this same way, the inukshuk can serve as a helpful marker for our understanding of how the core themes and stories of the larger biblical narrative hold together. Like the individual stones in an inukshuk, the key themes of the Bible are dependent upon each other. The stone pillars of *covenant* and *exodus* form the foundation. Indeed, understanding the architecture of the biblical narrative depends upon them. The voice of the *prophets* caps these two pillar themes because they so often recall the promise given (covenant) and the promise fulfilled (exodus) – promises central in God's self-revelation though human history. *Liberation* occupies pride of place, being both central and broad in its expanse. This stone resembles arms outstretched, an invitation to an embrace or hug. Liberation is the central theme that embraces the experience of the faithful from the beginning of the Old Testament through to the end of the New Testament. Understanding the meaning and mission of Jesus, for example, is deepened upon realizing that he both preached and embodied the kingdom of God that achieved its consummation and culmination in the *resurrection* experience. As we proceed, the inukshuk as a model for understanding the relationship between the key themes and seed stories in the Bible will come into sharper focus.

Below you will find a narrative outline for the Old Testament through to the New Testament. Familiarizing yourself with these narrative highlights in the Jewish/Christian story will help you understand the broad strokes of the story and give you a sense of their chronology.

A narrative outline

1850 BC	God makes a covenant with Abraham and Sarah. (Begins Genesis 12.)
1700 BC	Israelites are enslaved in Egypt. (Begins Exodus 1.)
1250 BC **Seed Story**	Exodus: God working through Moses liberates the Israelites from Egypt. God covenants with all of Israel on Mount Sinai (Ten Commandments). (Begins Exodus 19.)
1000 BC	Israel becomes a nation. (King David makes Jerusalem the capital.) (See 2 Samuel 6.)
921 BC	Schism: Israel (North) and Judah (South) separate. (See 1 Kings 12.)
722 BC	Assyria destroys Israel (10 northern tribes). (2 Kings 17:5-18)
587 BC	Judah defeated. Babylonian exile. Jerusalem Temple destroyed. (2 Kings 25:1-21)
520 BC	Return from Babylon. Temple rebuilt. Persia controls Palestine. (Ezra 1–6)
331 BC	Alexander the Great: Greek rule of Palestine. (See 1 Maccabees 1:1-9.)
167-63 BC	Maccabean revolt: 100 years of freedom. (Begins 1 & 2 Maccabees.)
63 BC	Roman occupation begins.
7-4 BC	Jesus is born. (Matthew 1:18-24; Luke 2:1-7)
AD early 30s	The conversion of St. Paul (Acts 9:1-19)
AD 70–95	The gospels are written.

When surveying the history of the Bible, consider these things:

1. *The relationship between God and the Israelites began with God's conversation with a clan or family (Abraham and Sarah).* Six hundred years later, following the great event of the exodus, God extends that conversation to all of Israel when God covenants with the people on Mount Sinai (Ten Commandments).

2. *Israel's sovereignty is relatively short-lived.* After a brief golden age during the time of King David, Israel is defeated by its enemies. Other than the 100 years of freedom between 140 and 63 BC, it is only in 1948, three years after World War II and the horrors of the Holocaust, that Israel once again becomes a sovereign nation.

3. *Jesus is born into a place and a time that has known oppression and poverty for centuries.* The Romans are just the most recent bullies to follow in the footsteps of the Greeks, the Persians, the Babylonians and the Assyrians. However, the great story of the Jews is one where God hears their cries and delivers them from their enemies. Jesus lived in a time of expectation of God's in-breaking into history and intervention on behalf of the chosen people: Israel.

4. *While the Old Testament covers events over a thousand years, the New Testament covers a very intense but brief period, no more than a hundred years.*

5. *Christians often use the adjectives "old" and "new" to describe the two covenants.* This can be misleading. The New Testament, or New Covenant, is not meant to express the notion of "new and improved," as if everything before it is now defunct or superseded; rather, Christians should understand that the Old Testament is the very bedrock upon which the New Testament is built.[16]

Reading biblical narrative: User-friendly guidelines

As we prepare to enter the biblical narrative, let us be conscious of these five points:

1. *God's word to us in the Bible cannot be separated from its historical context.* The place and the time in which God speaks does shape

the message, because the word is always given to us through human hands. So, as we read the Bible, we are always conscious of the history of the time and the cultural practices insofar as we can access them from our time and place.

2. *While the story of the Bible happened in history, biblical writing is not historical writing the way we understand it today.* The Bible is a story *in history* that has been interpreted through the eyes of faith.

3. *There is an architecture to the larger biblical narrative.* As we saw above, the inukshuk is a helpful image because these Inuit stone markers indicated safe passage, directions for travellers or caches of food in our far northern wilderness. The inukshuk can help the reader of the Bible remain oriented towards the key themes and stories that hold the entire narrative together.

4. *God's word transcends space and time.* In reading any given Bible story, we are always conscious of how God is speaking to our time and our place. This requires imagination and understanding about ourselves and about the world we inhabit.

5. *Finally, we go with reverence.* God's word is power to transform persons, peoples and the cosmos itself. Go with confidence. God is the promise keeper! Go with a sense of humour and humility. If God is love, then God's sense of humour must be immense – God understands that we're not always going to get it right. But we go anyway!

"Be not afraid": God is with you!

When God called Jeremiah, Jeremiah made excuses. "I am only a boy," he said. "I wouldn't know what to say" (see Jeremiah 1:6). While his hesitation is not uncommon for those who are called by God, the response God gives Jeremiah is worth noting: "Do not say, 'I am only a boy; for you shall go to all to whom I send you, and you shall speak whatever I command you … Now I have put my words in your mouth. See, today I appoint you over nations and over kingdoms, to pluck up and to pull down, to destroy and to overthrow, to build and to plant" (Jeremiah 1:8-10). Like Jeremiah, many of us will feel that the project is too big. God's word is too big! We will not be able to get our heads around it, let alone our hearts. But our sacred story is filled with ordinary folks who heeded the call of God and found comfort there also. Mary, long before she was crowned the Queen of Heaven, was a first-century Jewish peasant girl living in a small town far north of the capital, Jerusalem.

"Greetings, favoured one!" God says to her through the angel Gabriel. "Do not be afraid, Mary, for you have found favour with God." Then Gabriel goes on to describe how Mary will bear God's Son to the world, and we hear in Mary's reply an echo of Jeremiah's reply from centuries before. "How can this be, since I am a virgin?" Gabriel describes how the Holy Spirit will overshadow Mary, and how even Mary's elderly cousin Elizabeth has also conceived, "for nothing will be impossible with God." Mary is called Jesus' first disciple because of her response: "Here am I, the servant of the Lord; let it be done to me according to your word" (Luke 1:28-38). Her response is a model for us because it demonstrates a courageous and profound act of faith. We might say that Mary was saying yes to a teenage crisis pregnancy that – even in our day – would bring some tribulations, such as poverty, difficult questions or embarrassment. In her day it meant deep shame, expulsion from her family and community, and possible public execution. Yet, despite these dangers, Mary trusted that God would bring goodness out of a disturbing and deeply mysterious invitation to birth God's very self to the world.

St. Augustine once wrote that Mary conceived Jesus in her heart long before she conceived him in her womb.[17] Your courage in allowing God to speak to your heart through the sacred scriptures will also carry Christ to the world. Each of our lives is reflected and intertwined in the biblical narrative; in the following pages, we will explore how this happens. For as you gain confidence and familiarity with the sacred story, your life will proclaim the gospel.

Liberation

What is a "seed story"?

Both the Old Testament and the New Testament contain seed stories, that is, stories that guide and influence the interpretation of all the other stories.

For example, my childhood was chaotic. My parents married as teenagers when my mother found herself pregnant at sixteen. Alcoholism and immaturity weren't good foundations for marriage. After three children and ten torturous years, they divorced. My mother married another man who had a violent temper and his own story of brokenness. At seventeen, I fled the family home seeking peace and security. The night I made the decision to run away was an extended angry and searching prayer. I raged at God for the injustice of my life with the theatrical self-absorption of an unhappy adolescent. In the throes of this unravelling, God spoke to me of a radical alternative: I could strike out on my own. The reality of this option struck me like a hammer. Under a twilit Saskatchewan sky, I called for help. If God was calling me out, the Holy Spirit would have to guide and strengthen me. It was a moment of liberation. And every other significant event in my life from that point on has to be understood in light of the power of God to deliver a seventeen-year-old farm boy from a family life shaken by violence and abuse.

One of my students, Dan, has a seed story that is very different from my own. His home life was stable. His parents were committed to each other, and he speaks of great appreciation for the love and support they provided for him as he grew to maturity in a mid-size city in southern Ontario. Through the experience of growing up in such a home, in such a place and time, Dan chose a large university in a multicultural city in Canada. The more he learned about the world, about the marginalized and the broken, the more he felt a profound sense of God's grace. In gratitude for the life he'd been given, Dan reached out to embrace marginalized persons, especially young people. Their experience was not his, but the gift of love he had been given in his childhood strengthened him for the work of service in the world. God spoke to his heart. He wanted to give something back.

The seed story of the Old Testament: Exodus

The seed story in the Old Testament is a story of liberation. It is the story of God reaching into human history and freeing a band of Hebrew slaves from oppression in the land of Egypt. This story is recorded in the first fifteen chapters of the second book of the Bible, the book of Exodus. We will investigate this seed story in greater detail in Chapter 5, but you are encouraged to spend a few minutes reading or reminding yourself of this story (Exodus 1–15).

"Exodus" is a word that literally means "the way/road out of." Like so many words in the Bible, it is really a code word or a charged word that has many meanings: the way out of Egypt *into the Promised Land*; the way out of slavery *into freedom*; the way out of oppression *into liberation*. The experience of the Hebrew slaves who found themselves liberated from their slavery carried the story like a sacred seed with them. It became the story that informed not just their future but their past as well.

How exactly does this work?

Think of those *aha!* moments we have all had. This is the experience of the Exodus. For example, imagine a friend is behaving oddly for a few days. Something is different and you can't quite put your finger on it. You consider whether you could have possibly offended him or her. Then you get a new piece of information: your friend has discovered a tumour and only surgery will determine whether it is malignant or benign. With this information you can start to interpret the past – you see the events of the past few days with fresh eyes. And it begins to colour the way you see the future unfolding. It also informs your interactions with your friend in the present.

The exodus experience was just such an event for the band of Hebrew slaves who escaped from Egypt into the desert. For them, it was a faith experience of an historical event. It wasn't happenstance that they were able to achieve freedom. God was on their side! God was speaking through the prophet Moses to deliver them from their oppressors. Then, once they began to reflect on the meaning of their experience, they started to let this revelation of God's love for them guide their interpretation of their past experiences. The exodus became the prism through which they remembered and interpreted their long relationship with God. And they let the exodus experience speak to their present and their future realities as they saw them unfold.

The seed story of the New Testament: Resurrection

Christians have had a similar experience. When asked, many Christians identify the story of Jesus' birth as the most important story of the New Testament. This answer is likely influenced by the magnitude of the cultural experience of Christmas in the Western hemisphere. But Christmas is not the most important feast in the Christian liturgical calendar. Easter is! Others may identify the crucifixion as the most important story in the New Testament. They argue that if Jesus did not die for us, we would not have been saved. But if you think about this logically, the crucifixion cannot be the most important, because if the story had ended there, Christianity could never have been born. It is a bit of a chicken and egg debate: Had the women who went to the tomb following the sabbath to anoint Jesus' body actually encountered a corpse, Jesus would have been forgotten as one of the failed apocalyptic prophets and healers of his time.

Without the crucifixion, there is no need for a resurrection. Still, it is the resurrection seen in the light of the sacrifice of the cross that is the seed story of the New Testament. It is what theologians call the *paschal mystery*.

Everything depends upon it. The gospels themselves were written through the prism of the resurrection experience. The life and teachings of Jesus were interpreted through the lens of the resurrection. This means that the disciples who gathered around the story of Jesus were not remembering a past ministry of teaching and healing. They were experiencing Jesus raised to new life! In light of this reality of Jesus among them as a life-giving spirit, they came to their fullest understanding of his life and ministry, and his death.

Like the exodus story, resurrection is a liberation story. With the resurrection, Jesus was raised to new life, free of the bonds of death. Because of the resurrection, Christians proclaim their liberation from sin and death through Christ.

Liberation is a key theme in both the Old and New Testaments because it is core for the seed stories of exodus and resurrection; however, that does not make it an easy theme to master. Liberation or freedom can take on very different meanings for people in different contexts. For example, a person of colour in the southern United States during the late 1950s had very specific experiences of racial prejudice and economic injustice. The justice that Martin Luther King, Jr. and other civil rights leaders pursued was specific to their place and time. In our day, we might relate this to a teenage girl sold into the sex trade in Asia or Eastern Europe; she understands slavery and yearns for liberation in a different way than a middle-class teen living in a suburban neighbourhood in central Canada might. This is not to suggest that middle-class North Americans are immune to oppression or slavery, but that the forms these evils take may be difficult to identify amidst the distractions, entertainments and comforts of economic prosperity.

For example, many North Americans cite technology and its onslaught as a kind of bondage. The ubiquitous smart phone, whether tied to one's work or one's personal life, is a ceaseless call to connect or respond or relate without delay until there is never any downtime. Stillness, quiet without interruption, is almost impossible to find. The convenience of information on demand becomes a tsunami of digitized and wireless noise. Work never stops, and social connections beep, hum and vibrate until rest never happens. The quiet that self-reflection and a life of prayer and contemplation require is pushed aside by a wave that is too big and invasive to ignore. Whatever we have gained by the ease of connectivity with each other we are paying for by our slavery to micro-computers. Some young people in particular seem susceptible to the narcotic draw of incessant connectivity. Many teachers, from the elementary classroom to the college lab to the university lecture hall, have the experience of students unable to discern the appropriate use of communication technology. Affluent societies with access to resources like technology and other distractions are particularly prone to addictions that rob us of our humanity. Let us speak plainly: addictions are bondage. While the biblical narrative does not deal directly with Facebook or Twitter, it does have much to teach us about the slavery to things that keep us from the tender mercies of our generous God who wills for us freedom, peace and wholeness.

Of course, addiction to technology is only one example. Others include gambling, pornography, alcohol, pharmaceutical drugs, narcotics, gratuitous violence: anything that diminishes the fundamental dignity of humanity and creation that the biblical narrative envisions. We will return to the themes of liberation and oppression in greater detail in chapters 5 through 8.

Questions for reflection

In light of the seed stories discussed above, consider some of the following questions about your own life. You need not answer them all, as they are similar expressions of the same basic question.

- What is the basic story of your life?
- What is your seed story? Which story from your life has served as a kind of lens through which you've interpreted the other big events in your life?
- What world events have had the greatest impact on you?
- Was your childhood a happy one?
- Which of the stories of your life have been specially charged?
- The narrative of each of our lives vacillates between stories of hope and stories of despair. Has one or the other been more dominant in your life? If so, how?

Addressing these questions is the work of being an adult, but it is also how people of faith discern God's direction in their lives.

Passage for prayerful meditation

Find a quiet place to meditate with Psalms 104 and 105. These psalms praise God as author of all and acknowledge his role in the great seed story of the Old Testament.

3

Prelude to the Covenant: From Creation to Abraham

A rainbow in the clouds

The great American author and poet Maya Angelou spoke to a group of educators at a conference in Chicago in March 2013. It was a secular gathering of 140,000 educators from all over the world, yet Angelou took the metaphor she used to frame her keynote address from the book of Genesis. She said that teachers are the "rainbows in the clouds" (Genesis 9:13) for their students. Following the great flood that washes clean the corruption of the world, God places a rainbow in the clouds as a sign of the covenant between humanity and God. It is a promise that God will not condemn an imperfect world. It is a moment of re-creation where the old ways have passed away[18] and God is ever capable of doing something new. Angelou was reminding educators that the core of the student–teacher relationship lies in a promise. Teachers never condemn students. We challenge, cajole, support and love them into their giftedness.

In my present role as a vice-principal, when teachers send students to my office because of a conflict in the classroom, the student often begins with these words: "That teacher doesn't like me." This is a defensive posture that surfaces when a child feels judged. When reading the Old Testament, like the story of the Flood (Genesis 7), newer readers of the Bible often come to the same conclusion about God. The God we meet in the Old Testament often seems to be angry. In my work with teachers over the years, I have often fielded the question "Why is God so angry and punitive in the Old Testament?" This question likely arises because the stories that most Christians are familiar with are ones like Noah and the Ark and Adam and Eve in the Garden, stories where God – at least on the surface – seems to be meting out punishments, from wiping out everything in a great flood to making childbirth difficult for women because of the sin of Adam and Eve. As we explore a few key stories in the book of Genesis, we will look closely at this perception of an angry, judgmental God and reframe it within the larger context of the whole biblical landscape.

Neither does God condemn

One of my good friends, Beren, is an evolutionary biologist who studies fish. Every year, along with his family and some graduate students, he celebrates the anniversary of Charles Darwin's birth with a big party at his home. While my friend has no formal religious affiliation, he once shared this observation with me during a conversation about whether God exists: "When I am doing field research in Algonquin Park," he said, "and I am sitting up on a rock face above a lake in the night and the sky is lit with a billion stars, I know there is something. I can feel it. I just don't know what *it* is."

In many ways, Beren's experience is a universal one. It is the pre-condition or the prelude to the covenantal relationship we all have with sacred mystery: God. Many times in my vocation as a teacher, I have encountered students in their reflective writing or in conversation who have had their most profound religious experiences in nature: paddling a canoe through a moose-inhabited marsh, hiking through a white pine forest, standing atop a rocky mountain on a snowboard. God is revealed in nature. As humans, we have the capacity to know the great other that is both apart from us and one with us. Because we yearn to know what is behind the mystery of the cosmos and the mystery of our existence, our desire is to plumb the depths of this great relationship that marries our flesh and blood to the earth and sky.

Our Bible begins by addressing these fundamental questions in the first nineteen chapters of the book of Genesis. The stories contained in these chapters are some of the most memorable in all of the scriptures: the seven days of creation, Adam and Eve in the garden, Noah's ark, the Tower of Babel, the brothers Cain and Abel. These stories have been an enduring gift to the larger faith community for more than two millennia. While they are not historical writings in the way we understand history today (see Reading the Bible – User-friendly Guidelines in Chapter 1), they boldly proclaim religious and mythic truths that continue to inform and challenge our lives today.

Before we proceed, let us clarify some important distinctions between historical and mythic writing. There are still many Christians today who believe that the first nineteen chapters of the book of Genesis are to be read the same way we might read a newspaper, as if chapter 1 of Genesis were an eyewitness account of a historical occurrence. But the Bible is a library of books, and there are many different kinds of literature in a library. It is filled with many genres of writing, all filtered through the eyes of faith. The first nineteen chapters of the book of Genesis are more properly described as mythic stories. In our place and time, many of our students think of *myth* as a synonym for *dirty rotten lie*. If you are a teacher who has told a story in a classroom, you will have been asked, as I have been many times, "Is that story true?"

Usually, what lies behind this question is a bias that is part of our age. "Is that story true?" is a question about historical accuracy. The implication is that if the story happened in a certain time and place and it was witnessed, then it is somehow more true than a fictional story. Yet nothing could be further from the truth! Anyone who has read a great novel has had the experience of being moved by the truth of the story even if the details of that story were not historically true.

In the end, we are always more interested in what is the meaning of things than we are in documented unfolding of details.

Myth is not a dirty rotten lie. It is an expression of profound truth that transcends history. For Christians, the mythic stories that are contained in the book of Genesis continue to resonate with us because they contain profound religious truths that remain accessible to the contemporary faith community. The gauge for the truth of a story should be its ability to affirm and challenge our lived experience, not the historical veracity of its details.

We will look at three stories from the book of Genesis to explore why they continue to be embraced by the Church.

1. The seven days of Creation (1:1–2:4)

2. Adam and Eve in the garden (2:5–3:24)

3. Noah and the Ark (6:1–9:17)

Take a moment to read the two accounts of creation that begin the book of Genesis (#1 and #2 above). To say that these stories are not historical is not to say that they are not true. They contain very profound religious truths that continue to resonate with the lived experience of the Christian community.

First, notice that God is described very differently in the two accounts of creation. In Genesis 1 (1:1–2:4), God is transcendent, a kind of disembodied voice that speaks the cosmos into being: "Let there be light" (1:3). In Genesis 2 (2:5–3:24), God is described in anthropological terms, walking in the garden with Adam and Eve (3:8), creating with earth like a potter might. Very simply, with rich narrative details we receive two descriptions of the sacred mystery: God is both transcendent and immanent. The mystery that is God is able to be somehow beyond or outside the cosmos but also deeply present in it.

Notice how in Genesis 1, creation brings order to what is described in chaotic terms. Today, when we imagine what existed before creation, we imagine nothing: no light, no matter, no energy. In the biblical imagination, the authors imagined darkness, water, wind. God enters this chaos and brings order to it. In fact, Genesis

1 has an intrinsic order to the narrative itself. In simple terms, there are three days of separation, three days of population, and one day of celebration. This structure emerges from even a cursory reading of the story.

Here are some of the religious truths that are expressed in Genesis 1:

1. *God creates, and in doing so brings order to chaos.* When God speaks, things happen! God's word is power. Everything that God creates is good.

2. *We are made in God's image.* This means that all of humankind has a fundamental dignity and worth that finds its origin in God's power and goodness. It also means that God shares his power with us. We are co-creators. We have been gifted with the task of being stewards of God's creation. In the mystery of God's design, humankind finds itself in a kind of ascendancy over the created order. It is a sacred trust that has been given to us, to love and care for the natural world with its rich diversity of life and ecosystems.

3. *Even God rests after the work of creation.* Most of our students do not know that there was a time when malls were not open on Sundays. The need for rest and re-creation is foundational in human experience. Just like in athletic training, we must learn the pattern of stress and rest to make improvements in our growth, our strength, our vitality. We live in an age that encourages workaholics by encouraging a frenetic pace of daily life. Most teachers do not feel underworked. And many of our students describe their lives as stressful, with the demands of school and sports or dance and the myriad other activities in which they are engaged.

Genesis 2 is a very different kind of story from the first account. We might say that the story is framed around this question: Why are things as they are, and not as they ought to be? In other words, if God creates order out of chaos and everything that God creates is good, why is there evil in the world? Why do bad things happen?

Here are some important religious truths that we can share with students:

1. *In Genesis 2, God walks with us.* He forms us with his own two hands and breathes into us the very breath of God. In biblical terms, breath is associated with spirit. Our biblical ancestors, in observing their flocks, their herds, their own children being born, made this important connection: when a lamb or a calf or a baby is born, it has everything it needs to exist except for one thing – the breath of life. For our ancestors in faith, that first gasp of breath following birth was a gift given by God's very self. For each of us, it was our first experience of inspiration: literally an in-spirit-ing or in-drawing of breath. This is why the renowned religious educator Thomas Groome once told a large group of teachers that the best explanation of the name Adam he had come across is "a being alive with the very breath of God."[19]

2. *This mythic story explores the relationship between male and female.* While some interpret the creation of Adam and Eve as an acknowledgement that the man is primary and the woman is secondary, this would not be the reading of the story highlighted for us in the twenty-first century. Today, we recognize the truth that in the story there was no suitable partner for Adam until Eve was created. In other words, humanity was incomplete until Adam and Eve were united. This speaks to the deep complementarity between genders. "This at last," says Adam, "is bone of my bones and flesh of my flesh!" He might have said, "Here you are, my love; now I am complete!"

3. *The story in the garden explores our brokenness, our original sin.* In creating us, God shares some of his power. God does not make robots. God makes us free. We are given the power to choose. In the garden, God provides everything needed to survive and thrive, including the option to choose that which is not good for us. As soon as Adam and Eve choose the forbidden fruit, their eyes are opened and they know that they are naked. The consequence of sin is immediate. God did not punish them or smite them or make them feel small or ashamed. Sin is its own

consequence. This is a very important point, because this story has been so often misunderstood. Often God's description of the consequences of Adam and Eve's disobedience (3:16-19) is read as a punishment that is meted out by God. Today, we are sensitive to the distinction between punishment and consequence. Let us make the same distinction here. At the end of the story, God does not condemn them; he describes the conditions of their alienation from each other, from creation itself, and from God. In fact, it is God who clothes Adam and Eve before they leave the garden, a final act of care for his creatures who are living out the consequences of this own sinfulness.

The seed of a promise

When I read the creation accounts with students, I am always mindful to share with them that the biblical authors were not scientific thinkers. While they certainly used their powers of observation to describe how they saw the natural world ordered, their motivation was not scientific or historical as much as it was faith-based. Clearly, they were inspired to share their insights about the relationship between God and creation. Therefore, science and religious expression are not opposed to each other. They are different ways of knowing, different approaches to telling the truth of things. As teachers, we need to be explicit about this relationship, because it causes a lot of confusion for students as they grow through the stages of faith (see the Introduction). Similarly, when we share the story of Noah and the Ark, we must be mindful of where the stress points are – where to place the emphasis in the narrative. If we place the accent point on the fact that God initiated the destruction of humanity because he was angry at our sinfulness, then the image we leave children with is one of a wrathful God. This would be an inaccurate understanding from a biblical perspective.

If we examine more closely the story of Noah and the Ark, it becomes obvious where the accent points should be. First of all, the story is placed in the book of Genesis after the fall (Adam and Eve), after Cain kills his brother, Abel (Genesis 4), and before the Tower of Babel (Genesis 11). This section of the biblical narrative is often called the de-creation. It describes in rich, mythic descriptive detail the condition of things once sin has entered the world. God creates everything in goodness and for goodness (Genesis 1), but then the real consequences of human disobedience play out. There is brother murdering brother; there is excessive pride displayed by Adam and Eve and by the builders of the tower at Babel, yet God finds favour with Noah (Genesis 6:8). He works with Noah to re-create, to start again. And in the midst of this re-creation that was carried in the Ark appears the symbol of the rainbow that becomes the seed of the covenant promise. Following the great flood, God says:

> I have set my bow in the clouds, and it shall be a sign of the covenant between me and the earth. When I bring clouds over the earth and the bow is seen in the clouds, I will remember my covenant that is between me and you and every living creature of all flesh; and the waters shall never again become a flood to destroy all flesh. (Genesis 9:13-15)

The point of the story of Noah and the Ark is the promise, and it is expressed with a beautiful image. When clouds gather, and the storm is looming, and the clear sky is obscured by the darkness, there is God's bow, a brilliant arc of colour as a testament to the faithfulness of God to care for all of creation. It is an image and an idea that is repeated many times in the biblical narrative. In times of chaos, hardship or despair, God is present as the promise keeper and the life-giver. This is the religious truth we want to share with our students and our children.

Before we explore the importance of the covenant in greater detail in the next chapter, let us give the last word to Maya Angelou.

When she spoke to teachers in that jam-packed conference centre in Chicago, she praised them for their dedication to be an arc of colour in a child's sometimes cloud-tossed sky. The promise at the heart of the student–teacher exchange is a relational one that says, "I believe in you." Because the heart of learning includes the chaos and disequilibrium of not knowing, of not seeing clearly, students need to know that the teacher is the rainbow in the clouds of their imperfection, of their youthful ignorance, and of their developing characters. To be a rainbow in the clouds for students is to acknowledge that the student–teacher relationship is sacred and contains the seed of a promise. Religious educators who lead students through the Bible understand that God is the agent in all promises. Teachers reveal the love of God for all students when they live out of the good news of God's loving-kindness.

Questions for reflection

- What has been your primary experience or image of God: angry judge or loving/forgiving parent figure?
- In your life, who have been the impactful witnesses of God's love or God's wrath?
- As a teacher, how have you been the "rainbow in the clouds" for your students?
- In your own professional or private life, who has been the "rainbow in the clouds" for you?

Passage for prayerful meditation

Read God's promise to Noah: Genesis 8:20–9:17.

4

Covenant: From Abraham to Joseph

An introduction to covenant

Our faith story for the people of Israel begins with a husband and a wife who encounter God, whom they call *El Shaddai* (Genesis 17:1), in the very flesh of family life. Abram and Sarai begin a relationship with God that changes the trajectory of their lives, just as our encounters with God today can change the directions of our lives. Although nearly forty centuries have passed since their time, we share a faith ancestry that binds us together. Just as Abram and Sarai met El Shaddai in the messiness of family life, we too are nurtured in our faith in the everyday pains and triumphs of family life.

In our diverse, multicultural and multi-faith twenty-first century North America, Christian families – often by marriage, whether ecumenical or interfaith[20] – always seek the security of belonging that home and family provide. In this pursuit, God is not a peripheral player. Today, amidst the distractions of work and the frenetic pace of life in general, we sometimes feel that God is distant and maybe like us – busy with a million details. We might visit God at the church from time to time, maybe even every Sunday, but how often do we recognize God in the making of the lunches or the rushed dinner before the next basketball practice or dance rehearsal? Do we believe God is present while we negotiate whose parents will be visited for what holiday and, if our family is ecumenical or interfaith by marriage, which church, mosque, temple or synagogue we should attend?

Did you know that in our ancestral faith story, Muslims, Jews and Christians find common ground? A diversity of religious traditions is woven into the very fabric of our biblical faith. Similarly, in our ancestral faith story, God is not a distant, disinterested potentate, but an agent of loving power and promise who works through the challenges of family life in all of its diversity to bring us home, to bring us into secure and fulfilling relationships.

And it all begins with a promise.

Anyone who has ever heard the lament "But you promised!" understands the heart of the covenant. Promises are the glue of relationships. This is as true on a small scale between friends or lovers as it is on a larger scale between clans or families or even between nations. The strength and the "*endure*-ability" of any community depend upon the capacity of the members to be faithful to one another, to honour one another, to be dutiful to the other. In the everyday world of commerce and international relationships, we use words like *contract* and *treaty*. In the Bible, we use the word *covenant* for the sacred relationship that began between God and Abram/Sarai in the twelfth chapter of the book of Genesis.

Many Christians, when recalling favourite Bible stories from the Old Testament, will remember Adam and Eve in the garden, or Noah and the ark, or maybe the Tower of Babel. These stories, all found in Genesis chapters 1 to 11, are important because they are the primal or mythic accounts of the Judeo-Christian tradition. They introduce the flesh-and-blood promise that begins with the story of our faith ancestor's first contact with God. While we cannot call Abram and Sarai historical characters according to the standards that we use today to document and authenticate people and events, we do have a cycle of stories recorded in the book of Genesis that *stories* our tradition's earliest conversation with God; and with faith-filled imagination, we can hear God's word to us over the span of centuries.

Abraham and Sarah

The story of Abram and Sarai (as they are known when we first meet them in Genesis 12) begins with a call and a promise.

> Now the LORD said to Abram, "Go from your country and your kindred and your father's house to the land that I will show you. I will make of you a great nation, and I will bless you, and make your name great, so that you will be a blessing. I will bless those who bless you, and the one who curses you I will curse; and in you all the families of the earth shall be blessed." (Genesis 12:1-3)

God calls Abram and Sarai from their home and their family to a new place. Tied to this call *away* from what was comfortable and familiar to them was the promise of a blessing. Genesis 15 describes the covenant made between Abram and God. In the ritual of formally entering into a covenantal relationship, Abram is promised two important things. First, God promises that Abram will have many descendants (Genesis 15:5). Second, God promises that Abram will have land of his own (Genesis 15:18). In more familiar terms, we might say that God promises Abram a family and a home. In the 4,000 years that have passed since this first covenant, the value attached to home and family has not diminished. God calls each of us into relationship; God calls each of us home. Keep in mind, though, that these promises are grounded in the concrete realities of time and space. Encountering God the promise keeper in the flesh of family life includes the messiness of day-to-day living – washing dishes, changing diapers – and it includes the very real concerns of inhabiting space – mortgage rates, affordable housing, national boundaries.

Covenant always includes duties or responsibilities. *Testament* and *covenant* are words that can be used synonymously. In Chapter 2, we explored the seed stories of liberation that are core to both the Old Testament/Covenant and the New Testament/Covenant. The theme of covenant is core to the larger biblical narrative; it appears as one supporting stone in the inukshuk image. So we should ask ourselves, "What is the connection between the great stories of liberation and the cutting of the covenant?" We will explore the covenant ritual of cutting below, but the answer to the question involves the making of a promise and a barbecue.

Take a few minutes to read Genesis 15:1-21. It describes the covenant ritual between God and Abram. God promises Abram an heir, many descendants, and land. The promise of land from this covenant ritual later becomes the Promised Land to which the Israelites journey when they are freed from their slavery in Egypt. The ritual itself is an ancient one dating from pre-literate times. Today, we sign contracts to enter into binding arrangements. Think of all the documents that we sign to enter into contractual agreements: some are financial, like mortgages; some are relational, like marriages. Some of us formalize agreements with a handshake (like a bet during the NHL playoffs). Children will formalize agreements with a pinky swear. Even today, we have a variety of methods to seal agreements between persons or groups. These range from the legally formal to the folksy informal, but in every case there are consequences and repercussions for not keeping one's end of the bargain.

Four thousand years ago, in the era of the Abram and Sarai narratives, formal agreements were entered into by slaughtering animals, then laying the sides over against the other to form a path of entrails and sides of meat. Those entering the covenant relationship would each take a turn walking through slaughtered animals. Imagine yourself barefoot in the meat section of the grocery store without Styrofoam or cellophane! In Genesis 15, a flaming torch (representing God) passes through the trail of slaughtered animals. In ancient times this was the way to say, "If I am not faithful to this agreement, may what has happened to these animals happen to me." Quite literally, it was called *cutting a covenant*. ("Cutting" comes from the Hebrew word *karat*.) Following the ritual, a meal would be shared between the covenant partners. In these times before refrigeration, the eating of meat was much less common than today; therefore, consuming it was often tied to important events and celebrations, the way that roasting a turkey or a goose in our time is often associated with important cultural/religious feasts like Thanksgiving or Christmas.

The making or cutting of the covenant between God and Abram is a big deal. It is a binding promise that cannot be broken by time or circumstance: God is the promise keeper! Two things happen to mark the importance of this event. First, our faith ancestors receive new names. When we meet Abraham and Sarah in chapter 12 of the book of Genesis, they are known by different names: Abram and Sarai. Their names change as a result of their change of destiny. Encountering God in the making of the covenant changes the direction of their lives and ultimately their identities as well. (See Genesis 17:1-5; 15-16.) Abram becomes Abraham, which means "the ancestor of a nation" (Genesis 17:5). Sarai becomes Sarah because she "shall give rise to nations; kings of peoples shall come from her" (Genesis 17:16). Second, Abraham and all the males of his household and of his nation that follow are to be circumcised. Circumcision becomes the sign of the covenant. Sometimes the work of understanding the Bible involves speculation about motives for behaviour based on what we know of cultural practices during the biblical era. God offers no reason why circumcision should be a sign of the covenant, nor does the biblical author, but the practice does make sense on a number of cultural levels. First, it was a patriarchal culture, so it is understandable that males would undergo the responsibility of being covenant bearers. Second, circumcision is permanent, just as the covenant is binding for all time. Third, there is some symmetry between the cutting of the original covenant and the cutting that is involved in circumcision. Finally, one of the promises of the covenant is related to fertility (an heir, a large family, a nation), and Abraham and Sarah lived at a time when pruning was understood to be an essential practice to increase fruitfulness. For all of these reasons, circumcision does make sense as a sign or mark of a people set apart by their covenantal relationship with God.

The God of Israel made known to Abraham and Sarah entered into a special relationship with them. In simpler language, we might say that Abraham and Sarah began a journey with God approximately 4,000 years ago. For Jews and Muslims and Christians, this journey continues today because each of these world faith traditions traces its roots back to the person of Abraham. Since the Old Testament is the foundation for the New Testament, Christians with Jews trace their faith roots back to Abraham and Sarah. Similarly, the Arab world and Muslims in particular trace their roots back to Abraham and his slave girl, Hagar, who bore Abraham's son, Ishmael. Read Genesis 16. In our multicultural, multi-faith world, this connection should not be forgotten: Jews, Christians and Muslims have been in conversation with the same divine mystery since the beginning. Abraham called God *El Shaddai* (see Genesis 17:1), a Hebrew phrase that is traditionally translated as "God Almighty." This name is used for several reasons. First, according to the primal stories that were part of Abraham and Sarah's tradition, this was the God who, in the act of creation, brought order out of chaos (Genesis 1). This God was associated with mountaintops and therefore was transcendent, above things, in control. But at the same time, this God enters into relationship with the created order and all living things (Genesis 2). El Shaddai acts in human history with "an outstretched arm and with mighty acts of judgment" (Exodus 6:6).

When God covenants with Abraham and Sarah, God promises them descendants and land. As time passes, the promise is complicated by the fact that both Abraham and Sarah are getting old. Sarah is barren and post-menopausal (Genesis 18:11). The theme introduced here is one that recurs many times in the biblical narrative; that is, a woman is barren, yet God intercedes and brings fruitfulness to bear. The heir that God promises Abraham and Sarah is called Isaac, a name that means "he laughs" (Genesis 21:6). This is in reference to both Abraham's (Genesis 17:17) and Sarah's (Genesis 18:12) response to God's promise that a son would be born to them, even in their old age.

God's power is both *beyond* human frailty and *within* human frailty. The patriarch and matriarch cycle of stories in the book of Genesis proclaims to us a God who works through human fragility and weakness, with the power to keep promises. This first promise made to Abraham and Sarah is the foundation upon which we began to commune with El Shaddai forty centuries ago.

We have not exhausted the many stories of Abraham and Sarah found in the book of Genesis. Now would be a good time to read a few of them on your own before moving on to the story of their twin grandsons. Here are four suggestions:

1. Genesis 12:10-20: Abram and Sarai in Eygpt

2. Genesis 16: the birth of Ishmael

3. Genesis 18:16–19:29: the Sodom and Gomorrah story

4. Genesis 22: the command to sacrifice Isaac

For now, remember that their story begins our story in an important way. Following the primal stories of the creation, the fall and the flood come the Abraham and Sarah stories, which talk of God entering into a binding relationship with a family or clan. From the beginning, God is with us, promising home and family. God is the keeper of promises. As you familiarize learners with some of Abraham and Sarah's story, be mindful of how God may be speaking through their own family. If you are a mature Christian, then you are likely living out the faith of your ancestors. The gift of faith is one that is often nurtured in families. We are raised in the tradition in which our parents and grandparents nurtured us. Just as the Israelites could proclaim the God of Abraham (and Sarah), we can proclaim the God of our parents and grandparents. In the film *Simon Birch*, which is based on John Irving's novel *A Prayer for Owen Meany*, the narrator explains that he is a believer, not because of superlative catechetical instruction or Sunday school, but because of the Christian witness of his best friend, Owen. Nine out of ten people will respond that their faith today is a result of witness – someone we love who lives out their faith in Christ in a meaningful way that we have been able to observe. And we can make this claim with confidence from our experience – statistics are neither desirable nor necessary. This should give us comfort as religious educators. Our role is to build on a witness that learners have already received.

Isaac and Rebekah, Jacob and Esau

By the power of God, Isaac is born to Abraham and Sarah, despite their old age. Later, when the time comes for Isaac to take a wife, the theme of the childless couple is replayed. Although Rebekah is barren, God intervenes once again as the agent who brings fruitfulness to bear. This is a central concept in the theme of covenant: God continues to act to be sure that the covenant endures for always.

In response to Isaac's prayer (Genesis 25:21), God enables Rebekah to bear children, and she gives birth to twin boys (see Genesis 25:19-28). Since Esau is the older twin, the greater portion of the family inheritance should go to him. He is a skilled hunter, a man who can put meat on the family table. He is Isaac's favourite. In contrast, Jacob is portrayed as a "mama's boy," hanging about the cooking tents tied to his mother's apron strings. He is Rebekah's favourite.

Read Genesis 25:29-34 and 27:1-40 before you continue!

This next cycle of stories is about family rivalry, deception and playing favourites. The key message here is that God will not revoke the promise. Once it is made, it is forever, in spite of human frailties. Because Esau is the older son, he will receive a double share (or two-thirds) of the inheritance (see Deuteronomy 21:15-17) – double what Jacob is entitled to. Esau will also receive Isaac's blessing and take on the responsibility to be the covenant bearer for the extended family. Rebekah, however, has other ideas. After Esau sells Jacob his birthright for a bowl of stew,[21] Jacob is able, with Rebekah's help, to deceive his father and cheat his older brother out of his rightful blessing.

Notice a few things about this story. First of all, Isaac cannot retract a blessing once it has been spoken. Even though he was tricked into bestowing the blessing upon Jacob (one that was intended for Esau!), he knows he cannot take the words back. Most of us have had this same experience. If we say something cruel or spiteful, we may want to take the words back, but we cannot. The words, once they have left our mouths, are active in the world. In a sense, humankind made in God's image shares some of this power with God, whose words are action in the world: God *speaks* creation into being (Genesis 1). Secondly, Esau doesn't come off well in the story. There are a few reasons for this. In the long oral tradition in which this story was told, Esau becomes the ancestor of the Edomites: hairy, red rivals of the Israelites. When later generations heard this story, they knew the connection. Imagine them elbowing each other and exchanging meaningful winks as Israel (Jacob) bests the Edomite (Esau). At the same time, this is a story about how the younger and weaker prevail, not because they are somehow better, but because God is always working behind the scenes to bring the covenant promise to its fullness.

Read Genesis 32:22-32 before you continue!

As a result of Jacob's deception, the sibling rivalry intensifies to the point where Esau, the skilled hunter, wants to kill his brother. Jacob, in fear for his life, flees. Alone in the wilderness, the night before he confronts his brother and offers an apology for the wrongs he has committed, Jacob encounters a mysterious being. They wrestle throughout the night, Jacob insisting that he must have a blessing before he will turn the mysterious stranger loose. Jacob gets his blessing and receives a new name in the bargain. He will now be known as Israel because he has "striven with God and humans" (Genesis 32:28). Upon encountering God (or God's agent), like Abram and Sarai before him, Jacob receives a new identity. From this point onward he walks with a limp. Wisdom and experience are bought at a price. The next day he encounters his brother, Esau, and they are able to reconcile in a way that Jacob had not thought possible.

This is yet another story where God is able to work with human folly and deceit and transform it. The deceitful younger brother, Jacob, with time and God's work becomes Israel, the covenant bearer and father of the twelve sons who become the twelve tribes that form the nation Israel. Many of us can relate to these stories of sibling rivalry and familial conflict. Most of our deepest wounds are the result of the broken relationships that are part of our family story. Take a few minutes to remember old hurts (some may still be raw!) that originated somewhere in the complexity of your family relationships. Our Judeo-Christian story is one where God the promise keeper meets us in the misery and the majesty of family life. Catechists and religious educators help learners to see with the eyes of faith how God has been working in family, and with family and through family, to bring people to wholeness. Don't panic if this is difficult for you.

God works according to God's time, not ours. Consider the story of Joseph, the final character we meet in the book of Genesis. He waits a long, long time before he is able to see the hand of God working in his life and in the life of his family.

Joseph

The stories about Jacob's wives and his children can be found in Genesis 29 through 30:24 and 35:16-26. Joseph is the first of two sons born to Rachel and Jacob. This makes Joseph the second youngest of Jacob's twelve sons. Andrew Lloyd Webber's musical *Joseph and the Amazing Technicolor Dreamcoat* brought this biblical story to popular attention. Unlike the previous stories, which are about the patriarchs and the matriarchs, this one reads like a novella. It consumes the last fourteen chapters of the book of Genesis. Before you continue, take some time to re-familiarize yourself with the story. It can be found in Genesis 37–50. You might be surprised to discover that Pharaoh is not an Elvis impersonator in the biblical version! Dreamworks has produced an animated version of the story called *Joseph: King of Dreams* (2000), and for the most part it is faithful to the biblical text. It is an excellent vehicle for sharing this rich story with students or with family.

Joseph's story is important on a number of levels. First of all, in this story the promise continues in altered circumstances. It is through a younger son, not the firstborn who receives the greater inheritance, where God seems to be creatively at work. As in the story of Jacob and Rebekah, parents play favourites and there is rivalry among the brothers. This time, a favoured son, a little bit full of himself, is set against his envious older brothers. It is the story of a doting father who, in his old age, doesn't see the treachery in his own children. Given Jacob's own story of youthful deceit, the irony is striking. In the face of his sons' plotting against the favourite son, Jacob seems naive. But despite all of this, God is at work in the muck of family life, bringing the covenant promises to fulfillment.

In the story of Joseph, his gift for discerning the meaning of dreams is both a blessing and a curse. This is because Joseph is also a person of integrity who will not deviate from the truth-telling that is part of his gift. His brothers do not receive well the news that they will bow down before the younger son Joseph, so they plot against him, sell him to a band of slave traders, and convince Jacob that a wild animal has killed his favourite son. In his exile from home, betrayed by his own brothers, Joseph has only his faithful integrity and his gift to sustain him. More importantly, we are told that God was with Joseph (Genesis 39:2). This is a way of saying that other persons and other nations are blessed by their association with Joseph. This is a fulfillment of God's promise to Abraham that "in you all the families of the earth shall be blessed" (Genesis 12:3).

Joseph can discern the meaning of dreams. He remains faithful to God and faithful to his gift. He serves his Egyptian masters faithfully, even to the point of fleeing from the lusty wife of Potiphar who sought to seduce him. When falsely accused of rape by the vengeful wife, Joseph is imprisoned. Yet even there he is given the responsibility for the other prisoners by the chief jailer, "because the Lord was with him; and whatever he did, the Lord made it prosper" (Genesis 39:23). Eventually, Pharaoh hears about Joseph's ability to discern the meaning of dreams, and he calls for Joseph's assistance. In helping Pharaoh, Joseph helps secure Egypt's food stores during a severe drought. This does two things: first, Egypt continues to prosper even during a difficult time as her neighbours travel inside the national borders to buy food; and secondly, it delivers Joseph's brothers into his hands after so many years. Ultimately, after all the difficult years Joseph spent in exile from his home, he and his family are blessed not just with a reunion, but with a reconciliation. Joseph is able to recognize the hand of God moving through the life of his family. He is able to witness his brothers' regret for the mistreatment he suffered at their hands. Although he is able to lord it over them, as his dream had predicted so many years before, he does not. He forgives his brothers and is able to enjoy a tearful yet joyful reunion with his father, Jacob.

If you read to the end of the story, you will learn that Joseph is able to bury his father, Jacob, in the land of Canaan that God had promised them. And even though Joseph himself ends up buried in Egypt, he obtains a promise from his brothers that when their people return to the Promised Land, they will carry Joseph's bones with them to be buried with his family: Abraham, Sarah, Isaac and Jacob.

The covenant in family life

Like Jacob, Joseph is the younger son in whom God works to bring the covenant promise to its fullness. Despite all of the obstacles that present themselves in the flesh-and-blood complexity of family life, God remains the promise keeper, faithful always to the covenant. For our purposes, remember these important points:

- God covenants with a family or a clan long before the great seed story of the exodus takes place.

- God is the agent, the protagonist in the book of Genesis, who works in the muck and the joy of family life to honour the promises of the covenant. Human frailty (like barrenness or deceit) is no match for the boundless imagination and power of El Shaddai.

- Abraham and Sarah make first contact/covenant with God. Isaac and Rebekah bring Jacob and Esau, the quarrelling twins, to the covenant spotlight, where God is able to work with them until Jacob emerges as Israel, one step closer to the promise of a great nation. Joseph gets the clan into Egypt. This sets the stage for the great act of liberation and abundant life where El Shaddai reaches into the story of Israel.

When the book of Exodus opens, it does so with an ominous verse: "Now a new king arose over Egypt, who did not know Joseph" (Exodus 1:8). Soon after, the persecution begins. The Israelites will end up enslaved in Egypt for over 400 years before God responds to their cries of lament.

Questions for reflection

- In our long faith tradition, God often speaks through dreams. In our contemporary world, the influence of Jungian psychology continues to testify to the power of our dreams to communicate our heart's deep longing. Do you believe that God speaks through dreams? How could religious educators help learners discern the voice of God in their dreams?

- Amidst the painful and joyful history of family, how are you able to help learners see the agency of God working through family and with family to bring covenant promises to fruitfulness? Can you help learners to see the real estate God has set aside for them – in other words, what physical space is sacred in the life of a family? How can you help learners see how their ancestors have been a blessing? How can you help your learners in their mission of becoming a blessing to their families?

- By what name does God call your learners? How can you help learners see that their identity, their destiny, the trajectory of their lives is being influenced by their experience of God?

Passage for prayerful meditation

Find a quiet place to meditate with Isaiah 43:1-3 and Psalm 139:1-14.

5

The Exodus Story

Oppression

The book of Exodus begins with some ominous words: "Now a new king arose over Egypt, who did not know Joseph" (1:8). This narrative detail is closely followed by an ancient example of xenophobia – the fear of foreigners. "Look, the Israelite people are more numerous and more powerful than we. Come let us deal shrewdly with them, or they will increase and, in the event of war, join our enemies and fight against us and escape from the land" (1:9-10). Soon thereafter, Pharaoh enslaves the Hebrews to build his cities. Their lives are made difficult with hard labour. Pharaoh perceives the Hebrews as a great threat, so he attempts to have their male babies killed in order to reduce the possibility of an uprising.

This story calls to mind our own prejudices about the other. As religious educators we can ask questions like "Who in our world does not conform to our vision of what is acceptable?" Would it be the Taliban, the Muslim, the fundamentalist Christian, or the thoroughly secularized Christian? Maybe it's the single mother on social assistance or the homeless or those involved in the sex trade or the drug trade? Perhaps our prejudice is shrouded in ignorance. As an affluent nation in the northern and western hemisphere, do we engage in habits or cultural practices that are oppressive to people living in other parts of the world? Can we help learners claim these expressions of social sin? Can we help them move beyond the paralysis that can result from excessive guilt? Can we help them move beyond the despair that sometimes settles in when the problems seem too big to be resolved?

By helping learners understand this central "seed" concept of liberation, they will have some of the tools needed to grow into adults who, through a life of prayerful reflection, and a genuine search for truth, are able to recognize what in our lives is oppressive. The bullies and other oppressors of our school years often carry these behaviours into adulthood. Perhaps an addiction, like tobacco or alcohol or gambling, is the oppressor. It may be an unhealthy relationship in someone's personal or professional life. The person who gets under our skin the most can be an oppressor or a key player in an oppressive situation. Exodus teaches that God calls each person out of these difficulties into something better, something more life-giving and life-affirming.

God calls from the burning bush

In Chapter 1, we looked at how God called Abraham and Sarah out of their settled lives and led them to a new place. The same is true for Moses. It may also be true for your learners! Certainly when I left my family home at seventeen, I did not know exactly where it was that God was calling me. In reflection, I can see now many different moments where God's hand was guiding my decisions and actions. Faith educators and parents need to share their stories with children. God did not speak only to people in the Bible. Learners need to know that God speaks to each of us today as profoundly and passionately as ever. We merely need the ears to hear and the eyes to see. Jesus says this many times in Matthew's gospel (see 11:15, 13:9, 16, 43). Remember, Jesus made the blind see and the deaf hear so that they could encounter the kingdom. Moses' story is not so different.

Moses is considered the greatest of the Hebrew prophets because of his connection to the greatest of their stories. The stories of Moses' birth and youth owe more to legend than to history. We have very little historical information about him, and the stories we share cannot be called history in the way we understand history today.[22]

Read the story of Moses' birth and youth in chapter 2 of the book of Exodus. Notice how Moses ends up being nurtured and raised in the palace of Pharaoh. The wet nurse hired to care for him is his own mother! The original audiences who gathered to hear this story told and retold would have delighted in the details. Think of it: the greatest prophet and deliverer of the Israelites was being raised and nurtured in the palace of the arch-enemy, Pharaoh. The story of Moses would have been passed down through oral storytelling among clans and families for a few hundred years before it eventually became the *national* story concretized in the biblical narrative of the book of Exodus.

In his youth, Moses comes to identify with his Hebrew ancestry and kills an Egyptian who abuses a fellow Israelite. Soon the word gets out, and Moses must flee for his life from the power of Pharaoh. He escapes to the region of Midian and eventually marries Zipporah, the daughter of a Midianite priest. Moses tends his father-in-law's flocks and he and Zipporah start a family. A period of domestic and pastoral bliss follows, the duration of which is likely a few years. Then something happens:

> After a long time the king of Egypt died. The Israelites groaned under their slavery, and cried out. Out of the slavery their cry for help rose up to God. God heard their groaning, and God remembered his covenant with Abraham, Isaac, and Jacob. God looked upon the Israelites, and God took notice of them. (Exodus 2:23-25)

We can see quite clearly the link between the covenant promise and God's will to intervene. Suddenly, God calls to Moses from the burning bush. This is a key story for two reasons. One, it is the call of the greatest prophetic figure of the Hebrew story. Two, here God reveals God's sacred name to Moses. The story can be found in Exodus 3. Take some time to read it before you continue.

Sometimes we imagine prophetic figures as saints. We use the words as synonyms because we imagine them sharing a kind of elevated holy place that few can achieve. Prophets in the biblical narrative are known as *nabi* in Hebrew, which means "one who is called to speak for another."[23] Prophets speak for God. In the exodus story, God calls Moses from the burning bush to speak on behalf of God to Pharaoh. The message is simple: "Let my people go" (Exodus 5:1). Moses, like many of the prophets we meet in the biblical narrative, is hesitant to do God's will. He makes excuses: "I am a nobody. They won't believe me. I don't speak well" (paraphrase of Exodus 3:11; 4:1, 10). But as God did with the patriarchs, he does with Moses. God works with and in human weakness to keep the promise. God gives Moses a reprimand but also a helping hand. God says, "Who gives speech to mortals? Who makes them mute or deaf, seeing or blind? Is it not I, the Lord? Now go, and I will be with your mouth and teach you what you are to speak" (Exodus 4:11-12). God partners Aaron with Moses to help Moses speak, and God empowers Moses to work wonders in the sight of Pharaoh.

Finally, Moses does not want to confront Pharaoh without a calling card. Moses is a country shepherd and Pharaoh is the most powerful person in the region. "When I go to Pharaoh," Moses says, "Who should I say sent me?" God's answer to Moses requires some consideration. First of all, God's response in Hebrew is YHWH. Most scholars believe it was pronounced Yahweh, and that it could mean "I am who I am."[24] There is a tradition within Judaism that does not speak God's name aloud; rather, Jews would use the Hebrew word *Hashem* which means "The Name," or the word *Adonai*, which is the equivalent of the English word "Lord." Anytime you see the word Lord (always in capital letters) in an English translation of the Old Testament, you know that the original was YHWH. Since Jews do not speak God's sacred name, the alternate "Lord" is used. The question, then, is why do Jews not speak God's name and what can we learn from this?

First of all, in the culture of Moses' time, naming someone was the equivalent of having power over them. We should take note of this fact: in the biblical narrative, God reveals the name; Moses does not assign it to God. In a similar way, not speaking God's name gives reverence to God. God cannot be contained within a name. God cannot be completely known. God is mystery. The practice of not speaking God's name is a way for human beings to acknowledge this. Eventually, the first three commandments (see Exodus 20:1-11) will codify this understanding for all of the Judeo-Christian tradition: Do not worship other gods; Do not attempt to make an image of God; Reverence God's name. The practice of not speaking God's sacred name teaches a healthy respect for the awesome power of God. In Chapter 1, we acknowledged that the biblical narrative captures the long conversation we have been having with God. Embedded in the Bible is our unfolding, evolving understanding of God's revelation to humanity. In Exodus 6:2-3, God says to Moses, "I appeared to Abraham, Isaac, and Jacob as God Almighty [*El Shaddai*], but henceforth I will be known as YHWH [the LORD]" [my paraphrase]. Here the biblical author is letting the reader know that there is continuity between the God of the covenant promise to the patriarchs and the God of the Israelites enslaved in Egypt. At the same time, there is an increased understanding of the incomparability of God.

This story can help children appreciate the deep affinity between one's name and one's identity. The prophet Isaiah speaks for God: "I have called you by name, you are mine" (Isaiah 43:1). God speaks each of our names, and does so with loving dignity. Therefore, when we speak each other's names, we do so with loving dignity, since we are each created in the image and likeness of God. Most teachers have had the experience of confronting a child who is misbehaving. If they do not know the child's name and ask him or her for it, they are unlikely to get an immediate answer. Children know instinctively (and shrewdly) that if someone has their name, they have some power over you. As a teacher, when I approach a child or a teen who is misbehaving, I never ask for a name. First I say, "We don't know each other. My name is Mr. Olson. What is your name?" Nine times out of ten, the child will surrender his or her name because the power has been shared. Those of us who remember names of people we have met only a few times, or perhaps haven't seen for many years, exercise considerable authority. Remembering and speaking a person's name is a powerful gift. It engenders communion between persons. Because we are creatures and God is God, the Bible helps us to understand the divine–human relationship in our use of names.

Before we go on to consider the plagues and the Passover, think about the meaning of the burning bush. It is one of most powerful images in the biblical record. Moses is awestruck by the experience of a bush consumed by flames and yet not destroyed. In the same way, the Israelites were consumed by slavery and oppression but were not destroyed. The richness of the image of how God reveals himself to Moses should never stop us from recognizing the voice of God in our present lives. Many students and young people will ask, "Why doesn't God still speak to us like God spoke to people in the Bible?" The answer of course is that God *does* continue to speak to each one of us, but we must be willing to discern or investigate in the way that Moses did. He didn't turn away from the burning bush. His curiosity took him to an encounter with God. I offer this story to my students whenever we discuss the burning bush:

> On a sweltering day in June, I was in the drive-thru line at Tim Hortons. I was by myself in my minivan with the air conditioning turned on high, just idling and waiting for my coffee. Someone on a bicycle stopped beside the garbage can by the drive-thru window and started cleaning up the litter. It wasn't even his litter! And it was really hot outside: 33°C and humid. The person on the bicycle was wearing a T-shirt. It said ONE LESS CAR. God spoke to me that day. God said, "Park the van. Ride the bike."

I tell my students that I can't prove that the story is true. I have no documentation or authentication, no video or hard evidence. What I have is the memory of an experience that has been filtered through the eyes of faith. God knows my name. God calls me to a richer and more abundant life in harmony with the earth. God calls me to conversion.

Share your stories of the burning bush with your students, your children, yourself!

Plagues/Passover

The story of the ten plagues is well known to many who grew up watching Cecil B. DeMille's film *The Ten Commandments* starring Charlton Heston. More recently, many young people know the story due to the popularity of the 1998 DreamWorks film *The Prince of Egypt*. Even if you are familiar with these film versions, take some time to reacquaint yourself with the original. It can be found in Exodus 7:14–13:16.

Many contemporary readers of this Bible story (most of them liberals!) struggle with the image of God that they perceive is being presented. God "harden[s] Pharaoh's heart" (Exodus 7:3), yet God deals harshly with the Egyptians. Many people I speak with about this story find God ruthless. We know that we are at a great remove from the place and the time of the story when the audience is sympathetic to the antagonist! For the original audience of this story, the biblical author wants to convey that God was in charge of the entire situation from the beginning. God hardens Pharaoh's heart so that everyone gets the memo! No witness to the great event will be able to deny God's incomparability, power and sovereignty. At that time it was simply understood that God was fighting on the side of the Israelites against their enemies. In our time, at least one American president has claimed that God chooses sides in times of war.[25] So in some ways, things haven't changed very much. But, when reading the biblical narrative, we must always consider the original audience and context out of which the telling of the story emerged. Retrofitting our cultural and theological apparatus based on another time and place is often confusing and counterproductive.

It is also helpful to notice that the story of the ten plagues has a highly stylized structure.[26] In other words, a great deal of intent – theological and instructional – was part of the weaving together of this story. The first nine plagues are all exaggerated natural disasters that are narrated through the eyes of faith. We cannot overstate this fact. The miracle of the plagues is not that God intervened in the laws of nature to bring about the destruction of the Egyptians, but that the Israelites could see in these naturally occurring events the hand of God reaching into their lives to deliver them from bondage and slavery. The exodus story is not an impartial, objectively authenticated and corroborated historical event; rather, it is the collective memory of an event that has been interpreted through the eyes of faith. To this end, all memory is interpretation. Not one of us is in possession of an objective, non-biased memory. Let me use a story to illustrate my point.

Sister Hilda was my homeroom teacher in the seventh grade. She was also the school's vocal music teacher. In those years we began our day with the national anthem played on the classroom record player. We stood at attention and sang along. One morning, Sister stopped the anthem to announce that we were somehow in very poor voice and that she would have to start the record again. Only this time she would circulate throughout the class and if she touched a shoulder, that person was to cease singing immediately and sit down. I am convinced that this memory would have been lost deep within my unconscious except for the fact that Sister Hilda touched my shoulder that morning and, in doing so, single-handedly instilled in me an overly self-conscious, negative sense of my singing ability. When asked how many shoulders Sister touched that day, I am at a loss. I only remember one. All memory is interpretation, but with experience and wisdom we can learn to reinterpret a memory. I know now that boys' voices crack and change around the age of twelve, and that Sister *likely* touched a few shoulders that morning. I am not likely to audition for *Canadian Idol*, but I did sing my own children to sleep for years without giving them nightmares. In the end, all memory carries a bias, and we need to confront and claim our own biases.

With the story of the plagues, Jews and Christians throughout the centuries have consistently been able to see the hand of God working *for* the Israelites in the light of the covenant promise. And we let the power of that biblical memory help us discern the meaning of our present plagues as well. Although cautious discernment on the part of the believing community is necessary here, our sinfulness is understood as its own consequence. God does not need to condemn us. We condemn ourselves as we live with the consequences of our own poor and harmful choices. *Sin has consequences.* This is certainly the way that many interpret global warming. Be attentive to where the stress falls, though. God does not plague us with global warming to punish us for the excessive consumption of natural resources. *God condemns no one!* Rather, the sinful overconsumption of fossil fuels leads to the plague of global warming. This is very different from claiming, for example, that a certain population devastated by an earthquake is being punished by God for some transgression. Much human suffering is seemingly without reason and hidden in the mystery of God's will and purpose. But that fact doesn't forfeit the responsibility of the believing community to read the signs of the times and connect sinful human behaviour to plagues in the present world order.

The final plague, the death of the firstborn, is linked to the ongoing celebration of the Passover in the Jewish liturgical calendar. This is the culminating plague that touches the lives of the Egyptians and spares the lives of the Israelites. When the angel of death *passes over* Egypt at midnight and strikes "the firstborn of Pharaoh who sat on his throne to the firstborn of the prisoner who was in the dungeon, and all the firstborn of the livestock" (Exodus 12:29), only the firstborn of the Israelites who place the blood of the Passover lamb on the lintel and doorposts of their houses are spared. Since the Israelites were leaving Egypt the next day, they shared a roasted lamb so there would be no leftovers. They ate unleavened bread because there was no time to allow the yeast to rise. They ate bitter herbs to remind them of the bitterness of slavery. They ate with sandals on their feet and their staffs in their hands. In other words, this may have been history's first fast-food meal!

The differences between our fast-food meals and the Passover meal are obviously many. The Passover meal is infused with meaning. One might say it is the definitive meal of the Jewish experience, one where God arrives as the promise keeper and deliverer. Even today the Passover meal is the feast that celebrates and remembers and relives the experience of the liberation from bondage in slavery by God's mighty and outstretched hand. By contrast, fast food in the North American context is ruled by distractions and the frenetic pace of life. Our fast food is the experience of the tyranny of overconsumption and over-programming. If we remembered the Passover as history's first fast-food meal, we might as well begin to search for the meaning of inhaling quarter-pounders and gulping soft drinks en route to the next meeting or kid's activity. The deep communion of sharing food linked to memory runs to the very core of both the Jewish and the Christian experience. We will explore this theme in greater detail in the Chapter 8.

Crossing the Sea of Reeds

Most Christians are familiar with this story as the Crossing of the Red Sea. It is found in chapter 14 of the book of Exodus. The name "Red Sea" dates from the Greek translation (called the Septuagint) of the Hebrew text.[27] Many scholars believe that the crossing likely took place at "a marshy area of Lake Timsah or Lake Sirbonis farther to the north near the present-day Suez Canal."[28] There is an important point about the life of faith woven into the distinction between the Sea of Reeds and the Red Sea. In my experience, many Christians have difficulty letting go of the idea of a big splashy miracle. They want to see walls of water pushed back to reveal long banks of aquariums that the Israelites were treated to as they passed through the waters of the *Red* Sea. This is certainly the vision we get from films like *The Ten Commandments* and *The Prince of Egypt*. Somehow God must have overturned the laws of nature to lead the Israelites through the waters to freedom while the Egyptian army was destroyed. Certainly the biblical telling indicates something of the like. But remember, the biblical story is memory with a bias. Biblical authors remember events with the eyes of faith. The Israelites understood their escape through water from the force of the Egyptian army as the marvellous work of God. This is the dangerous memory recorded in the book of Exodus.

Two significant difficulties arise from our need to see a miracle of eye-popping proportions. First, if it happened that way for the Israelites, then why does God does not act in a similar way today? Those on the journey from child faith to adult faith ask this question all the time. Literalism in the life of faith is a kind of paralysis. If we operate from the premise that if the story is not literally/historically true, it is not true at all, and so we will not believe that God has acted in history and acts in the life of the world today. If one is bound by literalism, then how can one see God working? If one is paralyzed, how can one encounter the kingdom of God that Jesus constantly preached? The second difficulty is in making God an idol. If God can work only within my narrow human perceptual field, then I've made an idol of God that is as hard and inanimate as a golden calf or a bronze statue. I've placed God in a box. I've given God a name that binds. (See the discussion of God's sacred name above.) The miracle of the crossing is not that God could part the waters of the Red Sea; the miracle of the story *and* the genius of the story are that the Israelites were able to discern the hand of God working in their lives. How else to explain the inexplicable? How else to understand the marvel of their liberation from bondage in Egypt?

The desert/wilderness

From the comfort of an armchair with a full belly and a seemingly endless supply of municipal tap water that is safe to drink, one wonders how the Israelites could possibly complain to Moses when they reached the desert. They had just eluded the Egyptian army by escaping through the Sea of Reeds while being led by pillars of cloud and fire (Exodus 13:21)! Not long into their desert sojourn, though, the Israelites complain: "If only we had died by the hand of the LORD in the land of Egypt, when we sat by the fleshpots and ate our fill of bread; for you have brought us out into this wilderness to kill this whole assembly with hunger" (Exodus 16:3). Hunger and thirst are powerful motivators, as all consumers know. Those lower on the consumer food chain – the ones without safe drinking water or food as opposed to the ones at the food court in the mall – are most vulnerable. Here we might pause and gain a better appreciation of Esau's quick decision to sell his birthright to Jacob for a bowl of stew (Genesis 25:29-34). In this larger story of the Exodus from Egypt, the people are vulnerable precisely because they are hungry and thirsty. The desert is a crucible – a place where the people are subjected to forces that test them and make them change. And even in the people's extreme condition of deprivation and weakness, God is working. Two very important things are going to take place. First,

God is going to use the desert to teach the Israelites how to be *manna* people. Second, God is going to use the desert to form this band of Hebrew slaves into a nation.

Manna is a Hebrew word that means, "What is this?" The book of Exodus describes it this way:

> In the morning there was a layer of dew around the camp. When the layer of dew lifted, there on the surface of the wilderness was a fine flaky substance, as fine as frost on the ground. When the Israelites saw it, they said to one another, "What is it?" [*manna*] … Moses said to them, "It is the bread that the LORD [YHWH] has given you to eat." (16:13-15)

In response to the question "Has God brought us out into the desert to kill us?" comes the answer "No, God gives you bread from heaven." In the desert, God teaches the Israelites how to be *manna* people. God teaches them how to rely on God, how to trust in God's care and providence. For example, it was not just that God provided the bread, but that the bread was consumed in an atmosphere of trust. When there is scarcity, people tend to hoard. In the story, when people try to hoard the manna, it spoils. They must learn to trust that God will provide for them. This is a lesson that takes a generation of forty years. Forty in the Bible always implies a long enough time for something significant to happen. The experience of becoming *manna* people takes time. Over the span of forty years, all the elderly who entered the desert would have died there. Those born in the desert were raised there. Those who were young when the Israelites entered the desert grew to maturity there. By the end of their desert sojourn, the Hebrew slaves who entered the desert emerged as a nation that was governed by God. This nationhood was solidified on God's sacred mountain, the same place where Moses encountered God in the burning bush.

During their third month in the desert, Moses led the people back to Mount Sinai. In the past, God had covenanted with the ancestors of the Israelites. God had entered a binding relationship with a family or clan: namely, Abraham and Sarah and their offspring. Now on Sinai, *God covenants with all of Israel.* The story begins in Exodus

19. All of the people prepare for the ratification of the covenant by washing their clothes, keeping themselves ritually pure for three days (by avoiding sexual intercourse, which renders one ritually defiled for a day), and observing special instructions about keeping away from the place on the mountain where the power of God will draw near. In the same way that the people reverence God's name by not using it in everyday speech, so they respect the awesome power of God's presence on the mountain. Then, in a special ritual that involves animal sacrifice and the reading of the terms of the covenant (Ten Commandments) to the assembly, the people are consecrated, set aside for the special task of being God's people, a light to the nations. They give their assent to the terms of the covenant. To conclude the covenant ceremony, Moses takes the blood from the sacrificed animal and dashes half on the altar and half on the people, saying, "See the blood of the covenant that the LORD has made with you in accordance with all these words" (Exodus 24:8).

Sometimes the Ten Commandments (Exodus 20), with their traditional rendering of "Thou shalt not," sound foreign and accusatory to our ears. We imagine the commandments as God laying down the law from on high. From the Jewish perspective, the commandments are a gift of teaching. In the same way that God gives bread from heaven, God gives the people the gift of the Torah or the gift of teaching to help them become *manna* people, covenant people. The Torah proper consists of the first five books of the Old Testament: Genesis, Exodus, Leviticus, Numbers and Deuteronomy. These five books form the core of the Hebrew Scriptures, just as the Ten Commandments form the bedrock of the terms of the covenant. Later, those ten laws are expanded into a number of case laws. You can find them starting in the second half of the book of Exodus and continuing into Leviticus, Numbers and Deuteronomy.

The Ten Commandments are instructions for living the covenant – for living in right relationship with God and with others. The first three commandments focus on humanity's relationship with God, while the final seven concern our relationships with each other. Below are the Ten Commandments in their traditional language followed by the same law in contemporary terms. Sometimes updating the language used to express these time-honoured instructions can lead to a renewed sense of their gift to us.

1. I am the LORD your God; you shall not have false gods before me.
   Love God above all.

2. You shall not take the name of the Lord in vain.
   Acknowledge God's greatness. Avoid invoking God's name for selfish purposes.

3. Remember to keep holy the Lord's day.
   Make time for God.

4. Honour your father and your mother.
   Act lovingly towards those who care for you.

5. You shall not kill.
   Treasure life and protect it.

6. You shall not commit adultery.
   Be faithful in relationships.

7. You shall not steal.
   Respect the rights and possessions of others.

8. You shall not bear false witness against your neighbour.
   Speak with integrity and honesty. Avoid gossip.

9. You shall not covet your neighbour's wife.
   Be satisfied in your intimate relationships. Strive to develop healthy sexual attitudes towards yourself and others.

10. You shall not covet your neighbour's goods.
    Be satisfied with what you have and be happy when others succeed.

The Promised Land

The Torah ends with Moses on his deathbed gazing into the promised land (see Deuteronomy 34). Joshua will lead the people on the next leg of their journey. As the Israelites prepare to enter the Promised Land, they begin a new chapter in their long relationship with the LORD God. The family that entered into relationship with El Shaddai has grown into the people Israel. They are now a *manna* people who have been formed in the crucible of the desert, trusting in the LORD's providence and sworn to obey the terms of the covenant.

This nomadic people will have to fight wars to establish themselves in the land. Other charismatic leaders will arise. They will have to learn to be farmers. The gods and religious practices of their new neighbours will be a constant allurement. Israel will want a king like their neighbours; they will grow strong and rich. And when the people stray from Torah, God will choose prophets to call them back to the covenant.

God the promise keeper has drawn close to Israel, led her through the desert, liberated her and gifted her with land and prosperity. The future is bright! Finding the appropriate response to such a gift is the challenge for Israel. As their story unfolds, the people will once again find themselves in difficult circumstances. They will await God's anointed one (*messiah*; *Christos*) to once again restore their liberty and abundant life in the land flowing with milk and honey.

As we continue to explore the seed stories of the Old and New Testaments and their rich themes, we need to find time to rest in contemplation of them. Considering these themes *should* give us pause.

Questions for reflection

Before proceeding, think about how you can challenge learners with the following questions:

- Do I believe that God is active in my life, in this place and in this time, calling me to a more abundant life?

- Is God working in my life to release me from the chains of my prejudices, from the wounds and scars of my difficult times?

- Can I recognize my addictions, my neuroses, my issues enough to hear the voice of God inviting me to a land where milk and honey flow, which is to say a land where there is an abundance of that which gives life?

Passage for prayerful meditation

Read Psalm 119. It is the longest of the psalms, with 176 verses! The psalmist explores at length the blessings of living according to God's gift of teaching in the Torah.

6

The Prophetic Voice

Resting in the warm embrace of God who delights in our very being is easier said than done. The details of life often get in the way. For example, I may want to live out of the realization that God has gifted me with my family and a home and intends for me to come to some fullness in enjoying these things, but keeping big ideas like covenant and exodus (promise and delivery) in my working memory is a challenge.

Many folks find that when things are good, they are good by degree. And the degree to which they are good is determined by short cycles of time that are interrupted by the busyness of ordinary life. Bananas come home from the store wooden-green; suddenly, they are bright yellow and in that wonderful place between chalky and mushy. Too soon they turn the corner to brown-spotted and black-stemmed. For many, moments of grace come and go this quickly.

Life is filled with plateau moments of grace and contentment until the routines and duties of ordinary life drag us back down from the high plain. Life vacillates between celebration and routine. Sometimes, during the days that we naturally and necessarily fill with routine, we aren't able to recognize the fullness of the celebratory moments or events that have given us our very shape and identity.

In the Exodus story, soon after God has destroyed the threat of the pursuing Egyptians, the Israelites begin to complain to Moses that they would be better off as slaves in Egypt. There, at least, they would be saved from starvation in the desert (Exodus 16:3). The immediacy of hunger in the wilderness is a powerful force that fades the memory of relief and exultation that must have been part of the experience of fleeing from bondage in Egypt. It seems the Israelites had some trouble, like all of us do, remembering the stories we share that have grounded us and gifted us with our very sense of ourselves, of our identity and values.

To take two contemporary examples of this experience, the liturgical season of Advent and the feast of Christmas reveal how life in our present age can distract us from the genuine memory of what grounds us and keeps us whole. In the history of the Church, these two seasons have always been distinct. Advent prepares the community of faith to receive Jesus into our lives and hearts across time dimensions; that is, we remember Jesus entering human history in first-century Palestine, but we acknowledge that Jesus is present to us now, and we hope for Jesus to come in the future, as we profess in the Creed. But the frenzied pace of life in our turbo-technological, consumerist and post-Christian age has blurred the lines between preparation and feast. The waiting period of the Advent season is filled with shopping and socializing, blown budgets and list-making. In the past, the tree – a symbol of the Christmas feast – was put up on December 24. Now you see them in shopping malls and people's homes before the Advent season even begins. No wonder we find the trees unceremoniously dumped onto curbs on Boxing Day, barely thirty-six hours into the feast of Christmas, which lasts for at least twelve days. (Many churches celebrate the Christmas season up until the Feast of the Epiphany – the first Sunday after January 1 – but others may go to the Sunday following Epiphany. Some continue until the Feast of the Presentation of the Lord [February 2], which is forty days after December 25!) In the end, one wonders whether the purpose of Advent and the beauty of the Christmas season – which is a season, not a day – can be saved in our present age. If you want to be countercultural and preserve Christmas as a Christian feast, put the tree up late in Advent and keep it up until January 6, the Feast of the Epiphany.

Hope for the recovery of our collective memory and Christian identity lies in the imagination and initiative of our creative and tenacious God, who did not gift us only with covenant and exodus, with promise and promise fulfilled, without a plan to keep us mindful of the great stories and values that ground us. The power of God to remind us of our grounding stories is found in the voice of the prophets. This is as true today as it was in the biblical narrative. Hence, the horizontal stone slab in our inukshuk that connects covenant and exodus is the prophetic voice. It is important to keep in mind that covenant and exodus, with their rich narrative details and characters, are literally the stone legs or pillars upon which the entire biblical narrative rests. *Covenant* and *exodus* are the foundation. What we have established so far is that the experience of covenant and exodus get the Israelites to the Promised Land. These key experiences get us there, too.

There is a kind of plateau to this experience: a promise was made and, despite difficulties and hardship, pain and despair, the promise was kept. The Israelites emerged on the other side.

What does one do when one finally arrives in the Promised Land? As suggested at the end of the preceding chapter, practical considerations always follow the merrymaking and festivities that celebrate the beginning of a new and long-anticipated life. The Israelites had been in the desert for forty years. Recall that forty is a number in the Bible that always means *a long enough time for something important to happen*. When one arrives, one tends to settle down. We all know this is true. When we celebrate the wedding banquet, the exchange of vows, the entering into covenant, we go home and settle into married life – we establish routines. After graduation from high school, we go off to apprenticeships or college or university or community living and we settle in. We establish routines.

Our routines order us. There is a lot of discipline in maintaining our routines. While many people find comfort in the familiar structure of routine, others stumble over the monotony of it. Routine can lead to bleakness and breed complacency. We tend to forget the purpose behind what brings us our routines.

God's antidote to the problem of routine and shortened memories is the voice of the prophets.

In our earlier look at the prophet Moses, we heard that our English word for prophet means *one who speaks for another*. In Hebrew, the word is *nabi*. In other words, the prophet is one who speaks for God. And so, as we prepare to transition from our conversation about Old Testament key themes and narratives, we need to look carefully at who the prophets are, how they are called, their role, and what struggles and celebrations result from their work and ministry.

The call

In our collective experience of the mystery of God in the Judeo-Christian tradition, we understand God working in the context of promise and promise-fulfilled. If it is helpful, think of God as the CEO of a global conglomerate whose corporate vision is the fundamental dignity of each member of the organizational community, care for those in most need of support, healing for the natural world, and joy in the hearts of custodial staff and vice presidents alike. At times in the life of the organization, when the corporate vision is not being realized, who is God going to call? God calls the prophets.

The prophets are called to remind everyone in the community what the corporate agenda is, what the strategic plan is, what the key message is. Prophets are called to speak for God. They have been called in every age when justice is violated. They are called when the poor are disadvantaged. They are called when the widow and the orphan are not properly cared for.

Let us look at a few examples: some from the Bible and a couple from our contemporary world.

In the story of the Exodus, God calls Moses from the burning bush. Moses' reaction to God's call is in many ways typical of the prophetic call. First of all, God does not call Moses out of the blue, even though God does call in a lonely wilderness place. As we know from the biblical narrative, Moses deeply identified with the suffering of the Israelites, so much so that he had killed an Egyptian who had been abusing an Israelite slave (Exodus 2:11-12). When God called Moses, he was on the lam. He was in the witness protection program of his day. He had fled and started another life far from the injustice of Egypt. He had married and was working in the family business caring for the flocks of his father-in-law, Jethro (see Exodus 2:15–3:1).

When the LORD speaks to Moses from the burning bush and tells him that God had heard the people's cry, we know (as close readers of the biblical text) that Moses has also heard the cries of his fellow Israelites. Our psychiatrists tell us that if we do not deal with the past, it will deal with us. Moses had fled Egypt, but he had not dealt with the problem. He seethes with the injustice of his people's suffering at the hands of the Egyptians. So God calls him, commissions him and sends him back to Pharaoh. All of the prophets share a deep sense of God's justice for the world.

Another element of the call of the prophet is the usual first response of the one called. Moses hesitates to do God's will. Asked to speak for God, Moses feels he is not worthy. He makes excuses: "Who am I that I should go to Pharaoh?" (Exodus 3:11).

Two other biblical prophets have similar experiences. The prophet Jeremiah felt he was too young to speak for God, but God puts his very words into Jeremiah's mouth (Jeremiah 1:9). The prophet Isaiah is working in the Temple in Jerusalem when God calls him. His experience is described in Isaiah 6:1-13. Like Moses and Jeremiah, Isaiah feels he is unworthy to speak for God. In his vision, Isaiah has the experience of an angel taking a coal from the altar fire and touching it to his lips to purify his mouth. Catholics, before the proclamation of the gospel, make the sign of the cross on their head, lips and heart, saying, "Glory to you, O Lord!" Children's liturgy leaders teach their students to say as they do so, "May your Word, Lord, be in my mind, on my lips and in my heart." Like Isaiah, we believe that God does the work in making us worthy both to receive and to speak God's word. In conclusion, we see in the call of the prophets that God does not use a job description or reference a skill set when choosing those who will speak. We often hear contemporary preachers proclaim these words: "God does not call the qualified. God qualifies the called." This is a good description of the experience of the biblical prophets.

Besides feelings of unworthiness, there is another reason prophets are reluctant to accept the role that God is calling them to: the work is difficult and often dangerous. Again, Moses is a good example with which to begin.

The role of the prophet

When God calls Moses to go to Pharaoh and say, "God says, 'Let my people go!'" he knows he will be addressing the most powerful person in the land. In both biblical and modern times, prophets speak truth to power; that is, they speak the truth of God's intentions to powerful individuals who are in violation of God's will.

The role of the prophet is to call God's people back to the covenant. Prophets remind oppressed and oppressor alike that God's will is liberation and abundant life in the context of home and family. Return to the covenant – this is a call and a divine command to be in right relationship with others, with God and with the created order. It has two dimensions: to comfort the afflicted and to afflict the comfortable.[29]

When we read the prophetic books in the Bible, we see that the message they deliver from God always vacillates between comfort and challenge. There are tender words for those who are suffering and stern words for those who contravene God's intention of fundamental dignity for each person and a just distribution of the earth's resources.

With the wonders of technology and the gift of YouTube, we are able to enter the packed meeting hall and listen to Martin Luther King, Jr. give his final speech in Memphis on April 3, 1968. As the story goes, he had not been feeling well. But when he had received word that the hall was full and they were chanting his name, he got into a taxi and travelled across town to deliver what would be his final public speech. The speech is remarkably prophetic, because death threats had been coming regularly and he seemed to know that the end was very near. In fact, he was assassinated the very next day outside his motel room. Yet as death draws near to him, what is his response? He speaks truth to power: he reassures those assembled that the civil disobedience will continue despite governmental injunctions against them. Then he comforts the people with biblical language from the book of Exodus. He tells them that he has been to the mountaintop and has seen the other side. He has seen the Promised Land! "And I might not get there with you," he says, "but mine eyes have seen the glory of the coming of the Lord!" Despite threats against his own life, the vision of God's justice is so clear to him that, even in his final hours, he continues to afflict the comfortable and comfort the afflicted.

Though there is now a national holiday dedicated to Martin Luther King, Jr. in the United States, the American people did not always embrace him. When he first challenged them with the claim that their Constitution was not being realized in the day-to-day operations and relationships of their nation, many leaders and ordinary citizens found the message too difficult to accept. While there were many working in the civil rights movement, Martin Luther King, Jr. was its face and voice. It was a movement for justice, and he was the principal prophet. If we look carefully at the text of his great "I Have a Dream" speech, we find that it is filled with quotes from the biblical prophets. The dream of racial equality offers comfort for those who continue to suffer and a challenge to those who would stand in the way of change for a more just society.

Craig Kielburger, one of the founders of the international organization Free the Children, tells the story of a conversation he had with Archbishop Desmond Tutu of South Africa. Apparently, Craig was telling the Archbishop that he didn't like to read the newspapers. They were full of bad news, he explained, and this made it difficult for him to be hopeful in the midst of so many reports of disaster and injustice. Upon hearing this, Tutu challenged him: "What are they teaching you in college? Don't you know that the newspaper is a menu of the world's needs that God has delivered to your door for your convenience so that you can choose over breakfast the place and the issue that God is calling you to?" When Kielburger shared this story in a Toronto conference hall packed with Catholic teachers, he was also talking about another important attribute of the prophet. Prophets must be skilled at reading the signs of the time. They must be in touch with the world in which they live. They must read the newspapers, watch the news, speak with the people and immerse themselves in the unfolding story of the historical context in which they live.

Prophets must be forth-tellers more than fortune tellers. They are not so much predictors of the future as they are truth tellers about the direction in which current societal trends are leading. Prophets are skilled social analysts. They are people who are attuned to the suffering of others and who challenge those who hoard resources or services intended to be shared for the good of all. An intellectual understanding of inequitable social structures certainly helps in the prophet's formation, but this is not the most important factor. The prophets experience injustice in their bones. The physical experience of compassion for the child who suffers, for example, is so compulsively commanding that the prophet must act and must speak *against* the injustice and *for* the victim. Jeremiah, troubled by the persecution he is suffering because he spoke for God, simply decides to shut up. But it does not work. He says, "If I try to stop speaking God's word, then there is something like burning fire in my bones and I grow weary trying to hold it in" [paraphrase of Jeremiah 20.9]. For the prophets, God's word is fire!

When filmmaker Michael Moore accepted the Oscar for his 2003 documentary *Bowling for Columbine,* he criticized both the American presidential voting process and President George W. Bush for the invasion of Iraq. It was a disquieting moment at the premier event for the celebration of excellence in filmmaking in Hollywood, the epicentre of celebrity culture in North America. Moore was criticized for crassly bringing politics into a prestigious arts venue. In the supplementary material available with the DVD of *Bowling for Columbine,* Michael Moore defends his decision to speak out at the Academy Awards. His words are prophetic. He says he was tempted just to "soak up the love" and quietly receive an award that placed him at the pinnacle of his filmmaking career, but he felt compelled to speak up. He and his team were being recognized for challenging a culture of violence in the United States just a few days after the American military had invaded a sovereign country. Moore's speech was not popular with many, and he received intense criticism for the sentiments expressed and the timing of the proclamation. Although the video clip of Moore's Oscar speech is now available on YouTube, the Academy refused to make it available to the public for years after the event.

The role of the prophet cannot be romanticized. It is a difficult calling that often leads to criticism, hardship and, for many, death. Martin Luther King, Jr. was killed for speaking out about civil rights in the US in the 1960s. Mahatma Gandhi spoke for peace and tolerance amidst the tumultuous liberation and formation of India. He was assassinated by a fellow Hindu on January 30, 1948, on his way to a prayer meeting. Archbishop Oscar Romero spoke for poor farmers and labourers in El Salvador during a time of violent repression. He was assassinated while celebrating the Eucharist on March 24, 1980. Dorothy Day, one of the founders of the Catholic Worker movement, was one of the most influential Catholic women of the twentieth century. She dedicated her life to speaking for the working poor and feeding the hungry. While she was not murdered for her prophetic words, she did spend time in jail for various protests over the years. She lived out of a vow of poverty and entitled her autobiography *The Long Loneliness*. These are merely a few examples of prophets who emerged in the last century to speak truth to power, to comfort the afflicted and to afflict the comfortable. There are many others. And like the biblical prophets that came before them, these individuals remind us of our covenantal responsibilities to care for each other, to care for the earth and to recall the promises made, and the promises kept, by our gracious and generous God.

Discerning the difference between the false prophet and the true prophet can be difficult to do. As we have seen, the prophets are never self-promoters but come to the role with hesitation, often fearing they do not have the proper credentials. They know that the words they are compelled to speak are not their own, nor will they be popularly received. The prophetic voice always challenges the status quo and brings light to the darkness of greed, injustice, prejudice and oppression. The prophet is neither a predictor of the future nor a fortune teller, but someone who highlights the trajectory of sinful habits and harmful practices to help communities see the direction in which they are heading. To illuminate injustice, those who are called to speak for the voiceless or the powerless will use symbolic action. Jeremiah buried a loincloth under a rock after wearing it for several days without washing it. What remained of the ruined loincloth was a powerful symbol of what had become of Israel and Judah (see Jeremiah 13:1-11). Martin Luther King, Jr. marched in non-violent protest against unjust laws. Michael Moore took his film crew and two survivors of the Columbine massacre to Kmart to return the bullets that were lodged in their bodies. Jesus made a whip of cords and drove the money-changers from the Temple. In the gospel accounts of Matthew, Mark and Luke, this action precipitates the plot to murder him by the Pharisees and the Sadducees. Like all the prophets, the Jesus we meet in the gospels was criticized by the powerful, rejected in his hometown (Mark 6:4), betrayed and denied by his friends, abandoned by his followers, and publicly executed by Roman authority. Christians remember the story of Jesus through the prism of the resurrection experience, but embedded in the gospels is the dangerous memory of all those who mistook Jesus for a false prophet, a blasphemer, a madman.

From the perspective of the people portrayed in the gospels (see Matthew 16:14), Jesus was a prophet, set firmly within the prophetic tradition of Israel and Judah. When Jesus asks his friends who the crowds say he is, the answer is "one of the prophets." The first followers of Jesus experience him as a prophet with a keen eye and a sharp tongue when it came to hypocrisy, especially among religious elites. He also acts with compassion for the poor and the lame. His prophetic voice proclaims the good news of the kingdom of God, to which we now turn.

Questions for reflection

- Religious education teachers, like all teachers, must exercise a prophetic voice. In your role as a teacher, whom do you encounter who is in most need of comfort? Which persons or educational structures do you challenge in your words or in your deeds because they violate the fundamental dignity of the learner?

- Prophets are often criticized or persecuted. There is a profound vulnerability in speaking up against injustice. To what extent do you believe that God strengthens the prophet for work that is often messy, raw and risky?

- Jesus is a prophet. How has your encounter with Jesus in the Eucharist, in your prayer life and in the gospels prepared you for the work of speaking for the voiceless and challenging unjust practices?

Passage for prayerful meditation

Read Mary's Magnificat (Luke 1:46-55) – her hymn of praise and gratitude to God for the opportunity to bear God's son to the world. You will hear the prophetic voice in Mary's hymn as well as an endorsement of God as the promise keeper.

7

The Kingdom of God

I n Chapter 4, we considered the narrative history of the covenant relationship between God and the family of Abraham and Sarah and their descendants. Familiarity with this narrative history helps Christians to place the exodus event in the context of a long-established relationship between God and God's people. At the same time, it helps Christians recognize the movement of God in the lives of our own families.

Jesus himself was raised in a family context. Many Christians today in North America imagine a kind of first-century Jewish nuclear family (mother, father, single child) when they imagine the family life of Mary, Joseph and Jesus. However, based on the gospels and our understanding of Jewish culture at the time, this is probably very far from the truth. More than likely Jesus grew up in a large, vibrant and extended family.[30] His brothers and sisters are mentioned a few times in the gospels. While Catholic teaching sees these as cousins,[31] the fact remains that Jesus grew up in the midst of family life and all it entails. Because the gospels contain so few stories about Jesus before he began his public ministry, we cannot speak with certainty about what his childhood was like. But we can connect a few dots to create an impressionistic portrait of Jesus. As with a Monet canvas, distance from the time and place can bring the image into focus.

We have established that it is difficult to understand the significance of the exodus experience without understanding the narrative history of the covenant between God and the descendants of Abraham and Sarah. In the same way, we cannot understand Jesus except in the context of the Old Testament. Jesus would have read books that were part of the Hebrew Scriptures – what Christians call the Old Testament. The education Jesus received in his place and time (other than learning the trade of his father, Joseph) would have been a religious education in the synagogue. Jesus would have been taught to read, not so that he could go to college or university or achieve some standard of literacy, but so he could study the story of his people. According to the gospels, Jesus knew the Hebrew Scriptures well. They were life-giving for him. Here are three examples:

1. In the gospels of Mark, Matthew and Luke, Jesus is driven by the Spirit into the wilderness after his baptism. In the desert, Jesus is tempted by the devil. He resists temptation by quoting God's word (see Luke 4:4, 8, 12) from the Hebrew Scriptures, specifically the book of Deuteronomy. Jesus is strengthened by God's word.

2. At the beginning of his public ministry in Luke (4:14ff), Jesus selects and reads a passage from the prophet Isaiah to announce what his ministry is all about.

3. On the cross in both Mark's and Matthew's gospels, Jesus cries out, "My God, my God, why have you forsaken me?" This is the first verse from Psalm 22. While most Christians hear this as a cry of an anguished man suffering humiliation and excruciating pain, it is also an ancient prayer that is part of Jesus' Jewish cultural identity. In the agony of death, he was praying with the psalms. It is also important to note that although this psalm begins with an anguished cry (22:1), it ends with declarations of faith that God will deliver (22:31). During the pain of crucifixion, Jesus chose a psalm that is a profound testament of faith in that it recognizes God present even in the face of defeat and death.

The baptism of Jesus

After this upbringing, in which he was nurtured in the life of his family and the Hebrew Scriptures, sometime around the age of thirty (Luke 3:23), Jesus left Nazareth in Galilee and travelled to the south to receive baptism from John in the river Jordan. This experience altered the direction of his life. He had a powerful religious experience of the Spirit of God descending upon him and a voice saying, "You are my Son, the Beloved; with you I am well pleased" (Mark 1:11). Soon thereafter he retreated into the desert for forty days. (Remember that in the Bible, 40 is a symbolic number. It stands for a long enough time for something significant to happen. Jesus was in the desert after his baptism long enough for an important transformation to happen. Like the Hebrews who entered the desert as slaves but after forty years emerged as a nation, Jesus emerges from the desert to begin his new career proclaiming the kingdom of God.) Jesus emerged from the desert and then later, *after* John had been arrested, Jesus returned to Galilee and began his public ministry. The first words out of Jesus' mouth in Mark's gospel are these: "The time is fulfilled, and the *kingdom of God* has come near; repent, and believe in the good news." (Kingdom of God is most accurately translated as reign or rule of God.) We might think of this as a kind of platform statement, a crystallization of Jesus' life and mission. Everything that follows in the synoptic gospels is an elaboration of this statement. One might read it this way: "Something new is happening. God is close to you! Turn your heart towards God and accept this good news!"

On the one hand, Jesus is articulating his vision of God's reign. God is not stuck, according to Jesus. God's capacity for creative engagement is wonderful! "Here God is," Jesus says, "closer to you than you realize, maybe closer to you than your own skin. Allow yourself to accept God's love and God's mercy. This is good news!" This was a radical message in first-century Israel. Many were diseased; most were poor. What was once the great nation of Israel was oppressed by yet another foreign empire: this time it was the Romans. But despite all of this, Jesus was tuned to the frequency of God's love *for* and fidelity *to* Israel. Something magnificent and powerful must have happened to

Jesus during his baptism, because he came to understand that he had a unique role to play in the in-breaking of God's kingdom on earth.

Those of us who have gathered around the story of Jesus have come to understand his mission and person in a very specific way. For Christians, Jesus is God present in the world in the community of faith that we call the Church, or the body of Christ. Jesus is God's very Word to us (see John 1:1). Jesus challenges the notion of an elsewhere God, a God who set the world in motion, and now watches from a comfortable distance. The God that Jesus addresses as Abba/Father is not a distant and judgmental emperor on a golden throne, but rather a loving and caring parent figure who intimately knows and loves him. The faith story that Jesus was raised with is one where God is the promise keeper of the covenant, the one who is with Israel at all times. One of the promises of the covenant, a continuation of the promise to Abraham and Sarah, was that King David's "house" and "kingdom" would "endure" forever (2 Samuel 7:1-17). Remember, King David is celebrated as the greatest of the kings in the history of Israel. He lived a thousand years before Jesus, but the people remembered well the promise God made to David through the prophet Nathan. Remember, too, that the Roman occupation of Israel during Jesus' era represented only the most recent episode of bullying in the long line of empires that had oppressed the Jewish people. Scholars debate how much of a messianic expectation existed during the time of Jesus, but certainly John the Baptist was a *messianic* prophet. According to the gospels, John identified Jesus as the one in whom Israel's messianic expectation would be realized – that is, as the anointed one (Hebrew = messiah; Greek = Christ) sent by God to save or redeem Israel from its enemies.

The ministry of healing

John sends some of his disciples to Jesus to ask this question: "Are you the one who is to come, or are we to wait for another?" (Luke 7:20). Jesus answers this way: "Go and tell John what you have seen and heard: the blind receive their sight, the lame walk, the lepers are cleansed, the deaf hear, the dead are raised, the poor have good news brought to them" (Luke 7:22). For Jesus, his healing ministry gives witness to God's reign. In fact, Jesus heals as evidence of God's nearness and providence. When Jesus sends out the apostles to teach and to heal, he gives them these instructions: "Cure the sick who are there and say to them, 'The kingdom of God has come near to you'" (Luke 10:9). In proclaiming the kingdom of God Jesus heals a variety of ailments. Whether the ailment is an unclean spirit, leprosy or paralysis, in every instance the people respond in faith and awe at Jesus' healing authority – an authority that has its source in the power of the reign of God.

Let's look at three specific examples of Jesus' healing ministry in the gospel according to Mark.

The first healing is of a man with an unclean spirit (1:21-28). In the synoptic gospels of Matthew, Mark and Luke,[32] Jesus casts out many unclean spirits. Exorcisms were common in Jesus' time. Today, medical science and psychology have a variety of clinical diagnoses for conditions once thought to be demon possession. What is perhaps most interesting about this healing is that the spirit is the first one to recognize Jesus for who he is. The unclean spirit challenges Jesus: "What have you to do with us? Have you come to destroy us? I know who you are, the Holy One of God." This happens while Jesus is teaching in the synagogue on the sabbath. Although the crowd is "astounded" at his teaching because "he taught them as one having authority," they become more awestruck when Jesus is able to "command even the unclean spirits." With this healing, Jesus' authority over the forces of evil is made manifest. On a cosmic level, the reign of God is being born into the world through the mission and healing of Jesus.

Jesus also heals in the messiness of the everyday world. At that time, skin diseases of all types were known as leprosy. Those afflicted were made to leave their communities, keep away from others, and cry out, "Unclean, unclean," if anyone were to get too close. Mark 1:40-45 tells us that Jesus was "moved with pity" when the leper approached him with an appeal: "If you choose, you can make me clean." In choosing to help the man, Jesus reaches out and touches him, an unheard-of act given the purity laws that existed in first-century Israel.[33] The healing of the leprosy is "immediate," a testament again to Jesus' authority and power. And while Jesus "sternly warns" the man to say nothing except to show himself to the priest so he can return to his community, the man "spreads the word" so that Jesus' reputation grows and he can no longer go freely into the towns without crowds gathering. This healing further demonstrates Jesus' power, but also his compassion and his willingness to violate social customs to restore someone to community.

Those who seek the kingdom of God require some basic human wholeness. Someone tormented by evil is not free to consider the kingdom. A social outcast with a leprous skin disease who is outside of his or her community cannot seek the kingdom in isolation. In the same way, someone who is stuck or paralyzed cannot enter the kingdom. And so in Mark 2:3-12, Jesus heals a paralytic. (This story is also recorded in Luke 5:17-26 and Matthew 9:1-8.) In our time we might call this an intervention. Friends of a paralyzed man cannot reach Jesus because of the sheer size of the crowd he is teaching. In desperation, they remove roof tiles from above him so they can lower their friend through the opening. Jesus responds to this demonstration of faith, but not by administering painkillers or by chiropractic treatment. Instead, he forgives the sins of the paralyzed man. In doing so he introduces a controversy. Some scribes (interpreters of the law) who were present objected to Jesus forgiving sins. That was God's work! But Jesus asks a question: "Which is easier, to say to the paralytic, 'Your sins are forgiven,' or to say, 'Stand up and take your mat and walk'?" Then, to demonstrate his authority to forgive sins, he heals the paralytic, who "immediately" stood up and went home. If Jesus has the authority to heal a paralyzed man, he certainly has the authority to forgive sins. In the end, the crowd goes wild! They glorify God and testify, "We have never seen anything like this!"

In summary, Jesus' healing ministry is both a preparation *for* and evidence *of* the in-breaking or dawning of the kingdom of God. Those who are broken must be made whole. Evil is overcome, the isolated are returned to their communities, and those paralyzed by sin and harmful choices are forgiven. The kingdom is made visible when we are able to see with the eyes of faith as did the men who brought their paralyzed friend to Jesus. The leper believed that Jesus could heal if he willed it. Even in the spirit world, the demons are powerless against the authority of Jesus, the "Holy One of God." What we should not forget is that Jesus often healed people when he was going about the business of teaching. The ministry of teaching was also an occasion for inviting people into a greater awareness of the kingdom of God.

The ministry of teaching: Parables

Certainly in the synoptic tradition of Mark, Matthew and Luke, Jesus teaches primarily with parables. A parable is a story that compares something familiar with something elusive. By placing these two images alongside (literally, *parable*) each other, the listener is invited to see reality in a new way and is challenged to act accordingly. Because Jesus lived at a time when people lived close to the earth – farming and preparing food from scratch – he used many agricultural images in his parables. Jesus would take a familiar image from everyday life – vineyards, seeds, weeds – compare it with something else, and thereby invite the listener to see and act in a new way. Almost exclusively, Jesus' parables have something to do with the kingdom of God. While Jesus was not the first during his time to teach in parables, he used them effectively in proclaiming the kingdom. And he had to, because his vision of the kingdom was elusive. This is because the kingdom of God is radically counter-cultural to the kingdoms of the earth. The struggle to comprehend Jesus' vision of God's reign is not restricted to first-century Israel; it continues for twenty-first century North American Christians as well. Essentially, with a parable Jesus says, "If you can understand this everyday object, then you can begin to see and experience the in-breaking of the kingdom."

A good example is the parable of the mustard seed in Mark 4:30-32: "With what can we compare the kingdom of God, or what parable will we use for it? It is like a mustard seed, which, when sown upon the ground, is the smallest of all the seeds on earth; yet when it is sown it grows up and becomes the greatest of all shrubs, and puts forth large branches, so that the birds of the air can make nests in its shade."

Jesus compares a mustard seed to the kingdom of God. He teaches that if you understand the mustard seed, you can understand something about the kingdom of God. Although a mustard seed begins as the smallest of seeds, it grows into something large and unwieldy, something that takes over a garden and provides shelter for nesting birds. This is a way of saying that the kingdom has awesome power. Just plant it, Jesus says. Plant the seed and watch it grow! Give the kingdom of God an opportunity and it will astound and amaze you. Look at a mustard seed and look at a mature mustard plant. Can you see the connection between the two? It takes faith and imagination.

With the parable of the Good Samaritan (read Luke 10:29-37), Jesus also makes a comparison, but this time it is between a lawyer and a Samaritan. Today if you look up *Samaritan* in the dictionary, you will find that the term is associated with someone who is good or charitable or neighbourly. It was the opposite in Jesus' time. Samaritans were despised. Their ancestral roots were with the old Northern kingdom (Israel) that was destroyed by Assyria in 722 BC (see the narrative outline chart in Chapter 1) and later became a province of the Persian Empire. Over time, a religious split developed: the Jews came to see the Samaritans as people who had lost their way and could not be trusted.[34] Jesus uses this prejudice to teach something about the reign of God. In Luke's gospel, the lawyer wants an accounting of what it means to love one's neighbour, so he asks Jesus, "Who is my neighbour?" Instead of giving a legal definition, Jesus tells the story of a man who is robbed and beaten and left by the side of the road. The people whom the lawyer would have considered morally upright and faithful Jews – the priest and the Levite – refuse to act with compassion towards the victim. They are probably too concerned about prohibitions concerning the impurity that would result from touching a corpse. So they do nothing. But the Samaritan, the one held in suspicion, is the one who acts for the good of the victim. The Samaritan was a neighbour because he acted with mercy. By correctly identifying the Samaritan, the lawyer condemns his own view of the world and his own actions. The parable is an invitation to be in the world in a new way. Under the reign of God, Jesus offers this reality: a neighbour is anyone in need. In the kingdom of God, you reach out to your sworn enemy with love and mercy – and with your wallet! The challenge for contemporary Christians is to make a connection between a Samaritan of Jesus' time and a despised figure from our own. For example, how many Christians in large urban centres walk around or avoid homeless people on the sidewalks? Like the priest and the Levite, we can often give "acceptable" reasons for not helping the homeless. The parable of the Good Samaritan continues to challenge us to see and act in the world in a manner consistent with God's reign.

Sometimes the meaning of the parable can be misconstrued if the single comparison woven into the parable is misunderstood.[35] Take, for example, the parable of the Talents (read Matthew 25:14-30 or Luke 19:12-27). The comparison in this parable is between the disciples of Jesus, who expect the kingdom to appear at any moment, and the servants in the story, who are gifted with a small fortune from their master (the equivalent of about fifteen years' wages for a labourer during Jesus' time). Unfortunately, many times the master in the parable is compared to God by contemporary listeners with erroneous results. Some read this parable as an endorsement of free enterprise. Because the master in the story rewards his servants who have made profits on the original gift, Christians today sometimes think God endorses investment capital and the profit motive. However, we cannot lose sight of the audience for the parable. They are disciples who are living with an imminent expectation of the reign of God. And what does Jesus say to them? While you have been gifted with the kingdom, do not live in fear of judgment. Live expansively. Use and share and develop the gift you have received! This is one of ways that Christians are kingdom builders, responsive to the vision of God's reign that Jesus taught.

In the end, Christians understand that Jesus' proclamation about the kingdom of God has both a present and a future reality. To express this, we say the kingdom is *already but not yet*. In Jesus' person and mission, God's reign is present, but the fullness of God's kingdom or reign is still to come. This is the sense in which Christians are kingdom builders. Jesus showed us that in our living and our loving, in our healing of each other, in our forgiveness and care of each other,

God is present and working. When the fullness of our desire to live in God as beloved sons and daughters (as Jesus did) is realized, then the kingdom comes to greater fullness. It is true that Christians continue to live with an expectation of Christ's return. We call this the *parousia* – the Second Coming. History will reach its fullness when Christ returns, but the date and time of such an event is shrouded in the mystery of God's purpose.

Before we embark upon a fuller exploration of the great themes of liberation and abundant life, we should summarize some key points about Jesus' proclamation of the kingdom:

- During his baptism by John in the Jordan River, Jesus has a profound religious experience that initiates his public ministry.

- The primary goal of Jesus' ministry is centred on proclaiming the kingdom of God.

- The primary mode of this proclamation was in Jesus' healing ministry and his teaching. Healing prepares one for the coming of the kingdom. Healing requires a response of faith, a desire to be made whole.

- Jesus' primary mode of teaching in the synoptic gospels is through the telling of parables. Because parables make a comparison between something familiar to the listener and something elusive, a parable is an invitation to see the kingdom and act in a manner that builds the kingdom.

- Finally, Jesus' proclamation of the kingdom of God is rooted in the Jewish understanding of covenant: God is the promise keeper who is *with* his people.

In Chapter 8, we will see that the reign of God is understood most fully in the events of Easter morning. Without the resurrection, God's kingdom is just a preacher's dream with some moral precepts. By exploring the key biblical themes of liberation and abundant life, we will see how the pieces of the puzzle fit together. Covenant and the kingdom of God, the two themes we have explored so far, are good soil for discerning God's purpose for our lives and for the life of the world to come. The experience of covenant was the soil into which the seed of the exodus experience was planted in the Old Testament narrative. Jesus' vision of the kingdom of God was the soil into which the seed of resurrection was planted in the New Testament narrative. Taken together, exodus and resurrection are the seeds, the roots, the depth structures of our Judeo-Christian tradition. These two stories frame our experience of God who continuously calls us to liberation and abundant life.

Questions for reflection

- Jesus proclaims a specific message about the kingdom of God in his healing and in his teaching ministry. What is the message about God that you proclaim in your service to young people? Is your message proclaimed more with words or with actions?

- Parables were the primary teaching strategy employed by Jesus. How would you describe your primary teaching strategy? Is it one in which the learner is invited to encounter Jesus in an authentic and personal way?

- Jesus was nurtured and strengthened by the word of God found in the scriptures. In what ways are you strengthened or encouraged by the stories of Jesus' healing and teaching?

Passages for prayerful meditation

Read Luke 13:10-17. This is a good example of a story about Jesus healing while he was teaching. Notice the words Jesus uses to heal!

Read Luke 15:1-10. These are the parables of the lost sheep and the lost coin. Whenever we are tempted to give in to frustration over a reluctant learner, these are passages we must return to.

Read Luke 15:11-32. This is perhaps the most memorable parable in the gospels: the Prodigal Son (also known as the Forgiving Father). It spans an emotional landscape from ingratitude to the wasteful spending of an inheritance to tearful reconciliation.

8

Resurrection

The promise of abundant life

In Chapter 1, we established that the seed story of the Old Testament is the exodus from Egypt and the key theme is liberation. For Christians, the seed story and the primary experience through which we understand the mission and meaning of Jesus is the resurrection. To understand the meaning of the resurrection, we make a distinction between resurrection and resuscitation. Resurrection is the transformation to new life. Resuscitation is the return to old life, like when paramedics use defibrillator paddles to jump-start the heart of a cardiac-arrest victim. The gospels and the Old Testament contain stories of resuscitation,[36] but only Jesus is resurrected. For example, when Jesus raises Lazarus from the dead, Jesus is returning Lazarus to his old life. Lazarus, however, will die again at some time in the future. In the synoptic gospels, raising people from the dead was part of Jesus' healing ministry to proclaim the kingdom of God, while in John's gospel the raising of Lazarus points towards Jesus as the resurrection and the life. When Jesus is resurrected, his whole person (body and spirit) is transformed to new life. Resurrection is the culmination and glorification of human life that finds its purpose and meaning in God, in whom "we live and move and have our being" (Acts 17:28). As discussed in chapter 7, Jesus' entire ministry concerned itself with this truth: God is for us, God is with us, God is drawing us to God's very self.

Exodus and resurrection are closely related theme stories in that both concern themselves with liberation: the freedom of the human person and the community that God wills for us. God reaches into the oppressive, death-dealing muck of our lives and brings us home. Yet we know from the book of Exodus that the journey home is not effortless. On the journey we still need to live with each other and go about the business of life in a manner that is respectful of God and of God's creation. The promise of resurrection is a specific kind of liberation: it is the liberation *for* abundant life. In John's gospel, Jesus says, "I come that [you] may have life, and have it abundantly" (John 10:10). Resurrection does not simply mean the spirit's teleportation to heaven after the physical body dies. Christians confess the resurrection *of the body*. Resurrection is a *now* event as much as it is a *future* event. Our transformation to new life begins with witnessing God's reign now; it comes to fullness in our union with God after physical death. The new life that Christians are called to is abundant life: present life in community with responsibilities and hard work and disappointments, but also joyful life in communion with others as a free gift from the bounty of God.

Today, we limit ourselves to a narrow understanding of life and death. We think only of the biological or physiological aspects: life is when we draw breath; death is when the attending physician pulls the sheet up over our face. The biblical understanding of life and death is much greater than this.[37] We can illustrate this point with the story of the raising of Lazarus (John 11:1-44). Many Christians today read this story as a kind of proof text (using a specific passage from the Bible to prove something) for Jesus' power to resurrect – to bring the corpse from flatline to upright and alert. While Jesus certainly does resuscitate Lazarus in the story, he does more than this. Lazarus is not simply returned to the land of the living; he is restored to his family and his friends who love him. Life, in the biblical sense, is about reconciliation and being restored to one's community and one's family. Death is anything that keeps us from full communion with our kin and our friends and our God. Notice the words Jesus uses at the end of the story: "Unbind him, and let him go" (John 11:44). Lazarus is liberated from the bondage of death not so he can simply draw breath again, but so he can return to his community, his friends, his family. Jesus has gifted Lazarus not just with life but with abundant life. Lazarus will die eventually. We all will. But in freeing him from death, Jesus has proclaimed the resurrection that begins to transform the present life in hope of the future one. Jesus says, "I am the resurrection and the life. Those who believe in me, even though they die, will live, and everyone who lives and believes in me will never die" (John 11:25-26).

God's word to us in the person of Jesus is life-giving. Through Jesus, our lives are transformed: "Resurrection is the good news that the banished, destroyed one, is the one (the only one) who has the power to create a new community in which the gift of life and the task of life are kept together in healing balance."[38] The journey of life is always fraught with challenges as we seek out each other and look after each other's needs. But Jesus understood that God gifts us with life that is made abundant in our communion with him, with each other and with God.

Passover to Eucharist

In the celebration of the Eucharist, the great seed stories of the Old Testament and the New Testament converge. In the synoptic gospels, Jesus is celebrating what Christians call the Last Supper with his friends. The final meal they share is the Jewish celebration of the Passover. Together they remember and relive their ancestors' liberation from slavery. During the meal, Jesus takes the unleavened bread, gives thanks, breaks it, gives it to his friends, and says, "This is my body, which is given for you. Do this in remembrance of me" (Luke 22:19). In doing so, Jesus establishes a new covenant (New Testament) built upon the foundation of the first covenant (Old Testament). While celebrating the powerful memory of God the promise keeper and freedom giver, Jesus himself becomes the Passover lamb. Through his blood, death and all that it entails will be kept at bay. Through the memory of his life and ministry, communities will gather together to become his body. As the body of Christ, the community we call the Church continues to teach and to heal, and the kingdom is brought to fullness.

Eucharist is a Greek word that means "thanksgiving." For Catholics, Eucharist is the most powerful prayer of the Church. The poet, Father John Shea, described the celebration of Eucharist this way: "Gather the folks, tell the story, break the bread, and change the world."[39] The community coming together is important because from the biblical perspective, life and community are the same thing. This can be difficult for us to understand in our culture of radical individualism. In the story of the feeding of the five thousand, the crowds gather around Jesus and he has compassion for them because they are like "sheep without a shepherd" (Mark 6:34; see also Matthew 14:13-21; Luke 9:10-17; John 6:1-13). First Jesus teaches them with parables about the reign of God and about their long relationship with God as *manna* people. Then he feeds them, but the context in which he feeds them is significant. The disciples report that there is not enough food for so many people. Even though there is not enough, Jesus takes what there is and gives thanks[40] (*Eucharist*). When he approaches the situation in this way, not only are the people fed but also there is an *abundance*! Once the people have been nurtured on God's word and fed with the *bread from heaven*,[41] they are ready to go out and transform the world.

This is why the celebration of the Eucharist is so important today. It is the life of the community. We come together to hear God's word proclaimed to us. We are reminded of our story from both the Old and the New Testaments. Then, we gather around the table to receive the body of Christ, and in receiving it the community becomes the body of Christ (1 Corinthians 12:27). The community that is the Church becomes bread for the life of the world. Like the apostles, we are sent out to proclaim and to build the kingdom of God! We celebrate the transforming power of the resurrection now.

The empty tomb

At the very heart of the Christian story is a dangerous memory. Jesus, God's anointed, died on a cross *outside* of Jerusalem, the holy city. The ministry of Jesus ended in abject failure. He was publicly executed by civil authority, condemned by the religious authorities, and betrayed, denied and abandoned by his friends. By an act of charity, his broken body was taken from the cross and placed in a new tomb.

During his ministry in Galilee, people had gathered around the person of Jesus. They were drawn to him. His ministry of teaching and healing was liberating for them. But immediately following his crucifixion, his followers believed the jig was up. This is clear from the gospel accounts. The women were going to the tomb to anoint his body early on a Sunday morning because he had died at the beginning of the sabbath (sundown Friday). According to their customs, they could not anoint his body until the sabbath ended at sundown on Saturday. So they made their way to the tomb at first light early on Sunday morning. They were expecting to find Jesus' corpse. They were worrying about practical things, like how were they going to move the large stone blocking the entrance to the tomb. When they arrived, the stone had been rolled away and the body of Jesus was gone. A young man dressed in white told them that Jesus had been raised (Mark 16:1-8). The women ran away, amazed and terrified, and didn't say anything to anyone. This is a fragment of a very dangerous memory. Jesus had been liberated from death! Could it be true? And if it was, what did it mean? What were the implications of this for the disciple community?

When we compare the four gospel accounts of the resurrection, we find that the details vary. Each account contributes something unique about the experience of Jesus' resurrection. There are two details about the story, though, that are consistent. First, it is always women who are the first witnesses. This is a curious fact, given the culture of first-century Israel. Women were not considered credible witnesses and could not legally testify in courts of law. Second, the tomb is empty. Jesus had been raised bodily, a point on which the gospel accounts are insistent: when Jesus later appears to his friends, he is not some disembodied spirit or ghost. He eats with them (Luke 24:43). He invites Thomas to touch his wounds (John 20:27). In being raised to new life, the reality of the resurrection has transformed Jesus into a new creation (Colossians 1:15).

Let's be very clear about this: everything the gospel writers say about Jesus is filtered through the experience of the resurrection. Not one word about Jesus of Nazareth would have been recorded except for the reality of the resurrection. For Christians, this is the key pillar of the faith. The dynamic and effervescent God that Jesus proclaimed is the God of the living. New life is possible. Jesus, intoxicated with his vision of the awesome and unquenchable fire of God's power, was vindicated, liberated, set free.

Resurrection is not just about the glorification of this flesh after it is corrupted by death. Resurrection is not just about the childish notion of the gates of heaven being opened by Christ ascended to heaven. Resurrection is about the new life that is present in the here and now. Alive in Christ is alive now! Resurrection is good news, but it always exists in tension between the cross of Good Friday and the empty tomb of Easter Sunday. Brueggemann expresses it this way: "Jesus and his people always live between *the banishment of Friday* and *the gathering of Sunday,* always between *the exile of crucifixion* and *the new community of resurrection*."[42]

This leads us to the birth of the Church at Pentecost. Again, there is a strong connection between the Jewish celebration of Pentecost, which traditionally takes place fifty days after Passover, and the Christian celebration. The Jews celebrate the gift of the Torah during Pentecost. Christians celebrate the gift of the Holy Spirit. In both examples, God's providence is manifest. With the gift of the Torah, Jews are given the terms of the covenant. They are given the gift of being God's people. With the gift of the Holy Spirit, Christians are strengthened for the task of being the body of Christ for the world.

Pentecost

Before I settled down to work this morning, I went for a run. It was a sweltering, humid June morning. Midway through the run, I *bonked*. This is the term runners use when the tank runs dry, when the system crashes, when you either pack it in or struggle through to the end. The experience of bonking is always painful, physically and emotionally. During the forty days after Jesus' resurrection, I imagine the disciple community that had gathered around Jesus during his public ministry felt a similar thing. The charismatic leader of the movement had been silenced. The movement had *bonked*. The apostles were in shock. Many had experienced Jesus as a life-giving Spirit, but to what purpose? Without Jesus, the disciple community was rudderless. How would they go on? Could they go on?

Jesus had promised to send the Advocate, the Holy Spirit, to strengthen them for the task of continuing the mission to proclaim the reign of God (see Luke 24:49 and Acts 1:4-5). The Acts of the Apostles (2:1-13) describes the Pentecost experience after Jesus' ascension into heaven. This completes the fifth movement of the Paschal mystery. The Pentecost experience speaks truth to power as the community that continues to gather around the story of Jesus is silent and frightened no more. Father Ronald Rolheiser, in his book *The Holy Longing*, outlines a spirituality of the Paschal mystery. The Paschal mystery is the truth that is discovered in the suffering, death and rising of Jesus. It looks like this:

1. Good Friday: "the loss of life – real death or loss"

2. Easter Sunday: "receiving new life"

3. The Forty Days: "a time for readjustment to the new and for grieving the old"

4. Ascension: "letting go of the old and letting it bless you, the refusal to cling"

5. Pentecost: "the reception of new spirit for the new life that one is already living."[43]

Suffering loss and continuing on in some new way are essential parts of the experience of the Paschal mystery. Good Friday leads to Easter Sunday. The Easter feast is one of great joy and merrymaking. But what happens then? Jesus' friends still had to deal with the fact that he was with them in a new way. The old way was gone! They needed to make adjustments. Who was going to lead? Who was going to teach and heal? To embrace the void that Jesus' death had created, they had to let go. Remember Mary Magdalene in the garden when she encountered the resurrected Jesus. He said to her, "Do not hold on to me, because I have not yet ascended to the Father" (John 20:17).

For new life to take root, one has to let go of that which is past. The flesh-and-blood Jesus was gone. The disciple community now needed to prepare itself for the commission it was about to receive.

On the day of Pentecost, when Jews were celebrating the giving of the Torah, the disciples of Jesus received the Holy Spirit. In this experience, they become the Church. With the gift of the Spirit, they are strengthened for the task of incarnating Christ in the world. At his baptism, Jesus had a powerful experience of the Spirit of God descending upon him. Pentecost is the same kind of experience for the Church. John the Baptist had said, "I baptize with you with water, but one is coming who is greater than I. He will baptize you with fire and the Holy Spirit" (paraphrase of Matthew 3:11). After experiencing a significant loss, no one lives out their mission in the world until they receive and accept the new spirit for the new life they have been given. Without Pentecost, the resurrection is a joyful feast, but without legs. Pentecost is the fresh legs of the resurrection. In the heat of the Stanley Cup playoffs, with the score tied in the third period, the coach starts to short-shift the lines. Fresh legs on the ice late in the game are better than tired ones. Fresh legs late in my run this morning would have been a welcome respite from the heat and the fatigue.

The kingdom of God that Jesus proclaimed – the reign of God that Jesus inaugurated – continues to be brought to its fullness. Something decisive happened in Jesus' resurrection. Something unprecedented took hold of the created order. With the gift of the Holy Spirit, the disciple community has been strengthened for the task of building the kingdom. God is for us. Christ is with us. The Spirit strengthens us. The life we have been promised is realized in a covenant community that works together to heal and teach. In this there is joy. In this there is abundant life.

Questions for reflection

- Where in your present circumstance do you find evidence of new and abundant life?

- How is the resurrection of Jesus making a difference in your life today?

- The paschal mystery is a process that requires time. Can you identify examples of different stages in your movement from "real death" to "pentecost" in your life?

Passage for prayerful meditation

Read the Resurrection of Jesus in Mark 16:1-8.

9

Other Voices

Throughout the previous eight chapters, we have explored the narrative architecture of the Bible with its seed stories and great themes: promises delivered and promises kept. Like the inukshuk, the themes of the Bible present a composite boundary marker that gives us direction on the journey of faith. The central protagonist in the story of the Bible is God. The central relationship is the one between God and God's people. For Christians, God's enduring love for humanity and for all of creation is most fully expressed in the person of Jesus. In our encounters with Jesus, God is revealed as the one who calls each of us by name, the one who loves us unconditionally and invites us to a banquet already prepared where we are greeted as beloved guests. The greatest challenge for the believer is to accept this truth: each of us is God's beloved, destined not to merely survive, but to thrive in the midst of the boundless love of God. To this end, the library that is the Bible has many volumes that explore our yearning for that which only God can give. These books provide the varnish that preserves the revelation of God's unfolding relationship with humanity. They provide nuance, flavour – a depth of exploration of the great biblical themes and stories. Let us take some time to explore how they enrich our understanding of the central themes and seed stories of sacred scripture.

Psalms

Just before I began to write this book, my wife gifted me with Sinead O'Connor's two-disc recording entitled *Theology*. Nearly all of the songs are inspired by the scriptures, particularly the Old Testament books, including the Psalms. A good part of this manuscript was written with O'Connor's album playing in the background; it wrapped my efforts in a balm of inspiration for the things that engage the soul, that draw it out into open spaces where communion with mystery is possible.

Music has the power to do this. The word "psalm" is taken from the Hebrew word for a hymn set to the music of an instrument like a lyre. Therefore, the book of Psalms is a collection of 150 poems that were intended to be sung like hymns. The psalms form the ancient prayers of the Jewish people; as we saw earlier, the psalms were close to the heart of Jesus. In the Catholic Christian tradition, the psalms are sung regularly during the Liturgy of the Word at the Eucharist. They are also used in the Church's daily prayer, the liturgy of the hours. Why do the psalms continue to occupy such an important place in the prayer life of Jews and Christians alike?

The Hebrew version of the Psalms is called *sefer tehillim* or Book of Praises, because the hymns praise God from a whole variety of human experiences. These experiences are not relegated to the past, but continue to resonate with contemporary people of faith. The content of the psalms ranges from praise and thanksgiving for God's majesty, power and wisdom to laments or petitions that cry out to God for shelter, safety or protection from enemies. There are wisdom psalms that detail how happiness lies in doing God's will. Some of the psalms were used in ancient liturgical processions or worship services at the Temple in Jerusalem. Others are historical psalms that sing of the wondrous deeds God has done throughout history for Israel and Judah. Taken all together, the collection of songs that comprises the book of Psalms creates a rich tapestry of music for the soul. Sister Joan Chittister puts it this way: "The 150 songs of praise in the Book of Psalms are a sweeping overview of the spiritual life that … express virtually the full range of Israel's religious faith. They are the universal story of the soul's pilgrimage through life."[44]

One roadblock that Christians encounter in reading the psalms is that they do not always understand the historical context out of which they were written. The psalms have been sculpted by the worldview of an ancient people who experienced the world in a way that is at times different from ours today. At times, the psalmist can be seen as echoing our own struggles, never doubting that God exists but often wondering at God's hiddenness: "O Lord, do not be far from me!" (35:22). At other times, the language of the psalms sometimes takes delight in the suffering of one's enemies: "Happy shall they be who take your little ones and dash them against the rock!" (137:9). This is raw sentiment that is bold in its expression and shows the depth of lamentation over the destruction of Jerusalem, the sacred city. While the image is startling in its vehemence against the enemies of Judah, it is an example of the emotional range of the psalms. They do move from anger and despair to awestruck expressions of God's creative power:

> For it was you who formed my inward parts;
> you knit me together in my mother's womb.
> I praise you, for I am fearfully and wonderfully made.
> (139:13-14)

When praying with the psalms, we should be mindful of the organic quality of language. As we read the psalms in the twenty-first century we know that these verses were composed thousands of years ago in an ancient language, Hebrew. If we are reading in English, then we are reading a translation of the original text. All who studied Shakespeare in high school know that even the English language over a mere four hundred years changes significantly. Most high school students rely on study guides to help decipher Elizabethan English written in iambic pentameter. Because language is organic, it does change over time. Because all translations are interpretations of an original text, the psalms can be rediscovered in modern translation.

There are many excellent examples that have been published. Here is an example of how Stephen Mitchell renders Psalm 4:

> Even in the midst of great pain, Lord,
> I praise you for that which is.
> I will not refuse this grief
> or close myself to this anguish.
> Let shallow men pray for ease:
> "Comfort us; shield us from sorrow."
> I pray for whatever you send me,
> and I ask to receive it as your gift.
> You have put a joy in my heart
> greater than all the world's riches.
> I lie down trusting the darkness,
> for I know that even now you are here.[45]

The Psalmist expresses faith in the goodness of God even in the midst of troubles. In fact, he recognizes that God is present in the struggle; he acknowledges that moments of vulnerability are encounters with the divine. For Christians, this is another expression of our central symbol of Jesus on the cross.

In the book of Psalms, we have an ancient prayer manual that has the power to speak across centuries and cultures to pick us up, to encourage us in our faith, to give expression to the movement of our souls. Whether we are singing them in the context of the liturgy or reading them in our morning or evening prayer, they have the power to nudge our souls into the mystery of the divine presence.[46]

Letters

A significant portion of the New Testament is given over to letters, a literary form that has gone electronic in our present age. How many of us still send handwritten letters that are delivered by a person employed for the purpose of carrying mail to its destination? We live in an age of email communication that moves at the speed of light and is seldom printed as hard copy. Luckily, no such technology existed in biblical times! As a result, the library of the Catholic Bible contains twenty-one letters. Most of these are attributed to St. Paul or his followers and were written to early Christians and Christian communities for a number of reasons: to encourage them in their faith, to continue to teach them about the meaning of Jesus and his gospel and, when necessary, to correct misunderstandings that arose about some teachings. The letters also serve to manage relationships over time and distance. Evangelists like Paul would found Christian communities, live with them for a while, teaching and healing as Jesus did, and then travel on to the next place.

In those early years after the resurrection of Jesus, the church was growing rapidly and there was much work to be done. The teachings about Jesus occurred by word of mouth. The gospels had not yet been written. Many of Paul's letters predate the gospels and because they are hard copy of the earliest correspondence between Paul and the communities he founded, they have become sacred scripture for us. In the letters, especially those written by Paul, we have an unfolding revelation about Jesus the Christ. Much of our present understanding about the meaning of Jesus' death and resurrection, for example, comes from these letters. They provide another layer of revelation about the nature of sacred mystery, rich in narrative detail and direct instruction. In contrast to the gospels in the New Testament, they give no details about Jesus' ministry of teaching and healing; rather, they explore the meaning of the gospel lived out in Christian community in the years following the resurrection. For this reason, the letters continue to feed our spiritual lives and challenge us in our contemporary communities.

St. Paul is a dominant figure in the life of the early church. Although he never met Jesus in the flesh, he did encounter the resurrected Christ on the road to Damascus (see Acts 9:1-19). It was an experience that changed the direction of his life. He had been "violently persecuting the church of God" (Galatians 1:13) as a Pharisaic Jew who was zealous about the law and the traditions of Judaism. While Paul never clearly states his motive for persecuting Jesus' followers, we can glean from his letters that he struggled with the idea of a crucified and defeated messiah. His encounter with the risen Christ turned him down a different road, where he was able to see into the heart of the Christian mystery: God comes to us in vulnerability and weakness to lead us to liberation and abundant life. Paul expresses it this way in his first letter to the Corinthians:

> For Jews demand signs and Greeks desire wisdom, but we proclaim Christ crucified, a stumbling block to Jews and foolishness to Gentiles, but to those who are the called, both Jews and Greeks, Christ the power of God and the wisdom of God. For God's foolishness is wiser than human wisdom, and God's weakness is stronger than human strength. (1:22-25)

St. Paul, by his witness as an evangelist for the gospel, and subsequently in his letters, becomes an apostle to the Gentiles, or non-Jews. In his public ministry, Jesus brought the good news of God's love for humanity from Nazareth to Jerusalem. He was a faithful Jew ministering primarily to other Jews, the "lost sheep of the house of Israel" (see Matthew 15:24). Paul takes the gospel of Jesus from Jerusalem to Rome, the centre of the greatest empire of the time. Paul is God's instrument. He helps the other apostles see that Jesus is a messiah for the whole world (see Acts 15). In his letters and those of his followers, the church is left with a gift of teaching about the meaning of Jesus' death and resurrection. In short, Paul teaches that when God raises Jesus from the dead, all of creation, not just humanity, is redeemed. This salvation is offered as free gift, as grace. The gift is available to all through faith in Jesus Christ and his gospel. Accepting the gift of salvation in and through Christ continues to be the mission of all Christian communities.

For teachers in Catholic/Christian schools, there is an additional gift in the letters that is instructive for how we minister to our students in faith-learning environments. In his letters to the Galatians and later the Romans, Paul makes a distinction between the law and the gospel.[47] For Jews, the Torah is understood as a gift of teaching that comes from God through the prophet Moses. As a trained Pharisee, Paul understood that the Torah or the law outlined the terms of the covenant: it taught God's people how to live out of the covenantal relationship they shared with God as his chosen people. When Paul received the gospel, he needed to reconcile the meaning of it in relationship to the gift of the law. Was the law of his ancestors now defunct? Had the law been displaced by the gospel of Jesus? Paul's answer is a resounding no!

In his letter to the Galatians, Paul teaches that "the law was our disciplinarian until Christ came" (3:24). Law and gospel work together. We need them both. The purpose of the law, though, is to bring us to the gospel, to allow us to receive the grace of salvation made possible in Christ. Paul describes how Christ unifies the church *through* the law *to* the gospel:

> There is no longer Jew or Greek, there is no longer slave or free, there is no longer male or female; for all of you are one in Christ Jesus. ... God sent his Son, born of a woman, born under the law, in order to redeem those who were under the law, so that we might receive adoption as children. And because you are children, God has sent the Spirit of his Son into our hearts, crying, "Abba! Father!" So you are no longer a slave but a child, and if a child then also an heir, through God. (Galatians 3:28; 4:4-7)

This is instructive for how we minister to children within our Catholic/Christian schools.

Paul's message becomes clear to teachers when we consider how law and gospel co-exist in our school communities. First of all, schools are law cultures. Law dictates that if x happens, then y will result. There are consequences for actions, both good and bad. Assessment works like this and so does behaviour. If students develop good learning skills, then we witness good achievement. If students behave in a respectful manner towards each other, then classrooms are safe and harmonious places to learn. Behaviour that is inappropriate is corrected with consequences that range from student/teacher conferences to meetings with parents to suspensions. Yet Catholic/Christian schools are also gospel cultures. Because of what God did in and through Christ Jesus, the future is filled with unconditional promise. This is the good news! All learners have inviolate dignity. The gift of salvation is a grace for all. In essence, as teachers our message to every student is this: You are beloved of God. Your relationship with Jesus will lead you into a life filled with abundance and joy.

The tension that fills our days at school is the discernment necessary to decide which the child needs in any given situation: law or gospel? For example, if a child harms another student on the playground, which is the appropriate response? We use the law, in this case the *Education Act*, to teach children appropriate behaviour. We hope that with an appropriate consequence, the child will learn to behave in a way that is more respectful of the safety and dignity of the other. But hopefully we never lose sight of the goal, which is to bring all of our students to the gospel. In my present role as a vice-principal, I mediate the tension between the law and the gospel all the time. In effect, what must be determined on a case-by-case basis is what is best for the child in every situation. Is it an application of the law or the embrace of the gospel? – we must keep in mind that the long-term goal is always the unconditional promise of God's love. Often, when teachers are feeling bruised by the behaviour of a non-compliant child, they appear in my office frustrated and angry. There is a look in their eye at those moments that reminds me of Jesus before Pilate, with the crowd shouting, "Crucify him; crucify him!" They want a swift application of the law. Yet sometimes, given the challenging home lives of some students, what is required is an affirmation, not a hammer; love, not vengeance.

The great gift we receive from the letters we find in the New Testament is the instruction on how to be Christian community. It is never easy. Yet we must continue to be prophets for each other, comforting the afflicted and afflicting the comfortable in bringing both law and gospel to bear in our schools. Let the letters be a model for us in how we manage our relationships. May every email we compose be an exhortation to live out the challenge of the gospel. Perhaps then some of us will find words that are eloquent and true. We will inspire each other as Paul has inspired the church. We will accompany each other and our students on a journey from childhood to adult faith.

When I was a child, I spoke like a child, I thought like a child, I reasoned like a child; when I became an adult, I put an end to childish ways. For now we see in a mirror, dimly, but then we will see face to face. Now I know only in part; then I will know fully, even as I have been fully known. And now faith, hope, and love abide, these three; and the greatest of these is love. (1 Corinthians 13:11-13)

Visions

Earlier we explored how God often speaks to biblical characters in their dreams. Dreams have long been an important revelatory medium for discovering sacred mystery. So have visions. In the Bible, God's will or God's message is received in the form of visions on several occasions. For example, in the book of Daniel, six chapters (Chapters 7–12) are dedicated to exploring visions that Daniel had while he lay in bed (7:1). Chapter 13 of the gospel of Mark contains a little apocalypse that refers to the book of Daniel. But perhaps the best-known and least understood vision in the Bible is the one described in the book of Revelation, the last book in the New Testament. Students often have many questions about the meaning of these visions and the purpose of the book of Revelation in the Bible. This is probably because there is always a lot of popular biblical fundamentalist musings about the end of the world that stem from a literalist reading of Revelation.

First of all, the book of Revelation is not a prediction about the end of the world. While it does concern itself with the end times, it does not offer an opinion on when that might be. The book of Revelation, like much of the book of Daniel, is a specific kind of literature. We call it apocalyptic. The word "apocalypse" comes from the Greek word meaning "to reveal," which is why this book is called Revelation. Through a series of visions that are given to a man named John on a Greek island called Patmos, God's will for the world is revealed. The visions John receives are filled with extraordinary images and coded messages. The message is coded because he is writing during a time of great persecution for the early church. Christians had suffered at the hands of Nero (54–68 AD) and continued to suffer persecution under the Roman Emperor Domitian (81–96 AD). In other words, Revelation was intended to be a closed book, one that was intelligible to the seven Christian communities that it addresses (see chapters 1–3 of Revelation), but was not intelligible to the Roman authority at that time. So if the book of Revelation is not a prediction about the end of the world, what is its message?

Principally, the message of Revelation is hope for a church that is under persecution. Because the visions described are filled with fantastic dreamlike imagery, we cannot read or understand the message literally. Symbolic imagery is not a chronological text. Meaning must be gleaned from the images on a vertical plane rather than a horizontal one. In other words, we must seek the deeper meaning of the image rather than try to read it from left to right (the way we do with the English language) as if there were a coherent order of events. For example, at the beginning of the vision, Jesus is described as "one like the Son of Man, clothed with a long robe and with a golden sash across his chest" (1:13). This is the resurrected Christ who is in command of the situation and standing amidst the seven lampstands that represent the seven Christian communities under persecution. When Jesus or God says, "I am the Alpha and the Omega" (1:8), the original readers of this book would have recognized the first letter (alpha) and last letter (omega) of the Greek alphabet. In other words, God is present in the exhaustive span of history, from beginning to end. The Romans are not in control; God is!

The book of Revelation goes on, using visions of dragons and beasts and plagues to say that there is a cosmic battle being fought between the forces of good and the forces of evil. In the end, though, the enemies of God are defeated and the book concludes with three chapters (19–22) that describe the victory of Christ at the end of the world: "Then I saw a new heaven and a new earth; for the first heaven and the first earth had passed away, and the sea was no more. And I saw the holy city, the new Jerusalem, coming down out of heaven from God, prepared as a bride adorned for her husband" (21:1-2).

Despite persecutions and hardships, the people of God are always vindicated, restored and redeemed. God continues to be the promise keeper of the covenant. Sometimes groups of students like to study the book of Revelation in greater detail and decipher the strange images and metaphors. There are many aids available to assist the teacher in walking with students through the book of Revelation.[48]

The larger message from this mysterious and engaging book is that God continues to work in the muck of our everyday lives, inviting us to clarity of purpose in our service to others. The message from Revelation that is relevant for our students is that although they may suffer persecutions like cyber-bullying or racial prejudice or poverty or mental illness, the God of all consolation continues to be in charge of all of life. The visions described by St. John in Revelation are intended to strengthen Christian communities to weather the storm of persecution, while patiently enduring – in faith – until God's reign of peace and justice bursts through.

Questions for reflection

- The Psalms are the bedrock of prayerful expression in the Old Testament. What forms the bedrock of your prayer life? What times or places constitute your most profound experience of communion with God?
- Do you feel that there is enough prayer in your life? If not, how can you remedy this?
- As a religious educator, how do you model prayer for children? Are you as mindful of different prayer styles as you are of different learning styles?
- During occasions when the discipline of a child is required at school, how mindful are you about the distinction between law and gospel?

Passage for prayerful meditation

Read 1 Corinthians 13, St. Paul's great hymn to love.

Conclusion

Teachers of Religious Education in a faith learning context are called to be prophets of the word of God. Like the prophet Jeremiah, they often feel they are not literate enough (or "old enough," scripturally speaking) to proclaim and explore God's word in the Bible with their students. When they are empowered – when they are emboldened by God's word in their mouths – there is no stopping them. The same is true for parents who wish to gift their children with faith by sharing with them the larger biblical narrative.

In the key stories of the Old and New Testaments, God calls us to freedom for abundant life. This call to freedom is a journey, and as on most journeys, the road is not always smooth. But the agent of life and love, the principal actor in the biblical narrative, is the promise keeper and the freedom giver. One cannot encounter the word of God without being transformed. In the midst of the hard work that is involved in building anything, especially God's kingdom of justice and peace, there is also joy and a sense of peace that surpasses all understanding.

For Further Reading

Anderson, Bernhard W. *Understanding the Old Testament.* 5th ed. New Jersey: Prentice-Hall, 2006.

Armstrong, Karen. *The Bible: A Biography.* Vancouver: Douglas & McIntyre, 2007.

St. Augustine. *De sancta virginitate.*

Bibby, Reginald. *Restless Gods: The Renaissance of Religion in Canada.* Ottawa: Novalis, 2004.

Boadt, Lawrence. *Reading the Old Testament: An Introduction.* New York: Paulist Press, 1984. [*Note*: a revised edition of this volume is now available: Boadt, Lawrence. *Reading the Old Testament: An Introduction.* 2nd ed. Revised and updated by Richard J. Clifford and Daniel J. Harrington. New York: Paulist Press, 2012.]

Boomershine, Thomas E. *Story Journey: An Invitation to the Gospel as Storytelling.* Nashville: Abingdon Press, 1988.

Borg, Marcus J. *Reading the Bible Again for the First Time.* San Francisco: HarperSanFrancisco, 2002.

Brown, Raymond E. *101 Questions & Answers on the Bible.* New York: Paulist Press, 1990.

Brueggemann, Walter. *The Bible Makes Sense.* Rev. ed. Cincinnati: St. Anthony Messenger Press, 1989.

————. *An Introduction to the Old Testament: The Canon and Christian Imagination.* Louisville: Westminster John Knox Press, 2003.

————. *Theology of the Old Testament: Testimony, Dispute, Advocacy.* Minneapolis: Fortress Press, 1997.

Cooper, Noel. *Language of the Heart: How to Read the Bible – A User's Guide for Catholics.* Ottawa: Novalis, 2003.

Copley, Terence, Rob Freathy, and Karen Walshe. *Teaching Biblical Narrative: A Summary of the Main Findings of the Biblos Project, 1996–2004.* Biblos Project: University of Exeter, School of Education and Lifelong Learning, 2004.

Crossan, John Dominic. *Jesus: A Revolutionary Biography.* San Francisco: HarperCollins, 1994.

Fitzmyer, Joseph A. *A Christological Catechism: New Testament Answers.* New York: Paulist Press, 1991.

Fowler, James W. *Stages of Faith: The Psychology of Human Development and the Quest for Meaning.* New York: HarperCollins, 1981.

Friedman, Richard Elliott. *Who Wrote the Bible?* New York: HarperSanFrancisco, 1987.

Groome, Thomas H. *What Makes Us Catholic: Eight Gifts for Life.* San Francisco: HarperSanFrancisco, 2002.

Johnson, Elizabeth A. *Truly Our Sister: A Theology of Mary in the Communion of Saints.* New York: Continuum, 2003.

Klein, Peter. *The Scripture Source Book for Catholics.* Orlando: Harcourt Religion Publishers, 2008.

Lukefahr, Oscar. *A Catholic Guide to the Bible.* Rev. and expanded ed. Liguori, MO: Liguori Publications, 1998.

McKenzie, Leon. *The Religious Education of Adults.* Birmingham: Religious Education Press, 1982.

Moran, Gabriel. *Religious Education Development: Images for the Future*. Minneapolis: Winston Press, 1983.

Mulligan, James T. *Catholic Education: Ensuring a Future*. 2nd ed. Ottawa: Novalis, 2005.

Nutting Ralph, Margaret. *And God Said What? An Introduction to Biblical Literary Forms*. Rev. ed. New Jersey: Paulist Press, 2003.

The New Jerome Biblical Commentary: Student Edition. Edited by Raymond E. Brown, Joseph A. Fitzmyer, and Roland E. Murphy. Englewood Cliffs, NJ: Prentice Hall, 1993.

Rolheiser, Ronald. *The Holy Longing: The Search for a Christian Spirituality*. Toronto: Doubleday, 1999.

Shea, John. *Stories of God: An Unauthorized Biography*. Leominster, UK: Gracewing, 1989.

Spivey, Robert A. and D. Moody Smith. *Anatomy of the New Testament: A Guide to Its Structure and Meaning*. 5th ed. Upper Saddle River, NJ: Prentice Hall, 1995.

Walther, Carl F. *The Proper Distinction Between Law and Gospel*. St. Louis: Concordia, 1986.

Endnotes

1   Terence Copley, Rob Freathy and Karen Walshe, *Teaching Biblical Narrative: A Summary of the Main Findings of the Biblos Project, 1996–2004* (Biblos Project: University of Exeter, School of Education and Lifelong Learning, 2004), 5.

2   James W. Fowler, *Stages of Faith: The Psychology of Human Development and the Quest for Meaning* (New York: HarperCollins, 1981), Part IV.

3   Gabriel Moran, *Religious Education Development: Images for the Future* (Minneapolis: Winston Press, 1983), 183–207.

4   Moran, *Religious Education Development*, 190.

5   Moran, *Religious Education Development*, 192.

6   James T. Mulligan, *Catholic Education: Ensuring a Future*, 2nd ed. (Ottawa: Novalis, 2005), 223–30.

7   The Biblos Project, led by Terence Copley from the University of Exeter's School of Education and Lifelong Learning in the UK, was initiated for the following reasons. First, the Bible had largely disappeared from Religious Education (RE). Second, teachers, especially in primary schools, were reluctant to address biblical material. And third, biblical material was being secularized at the classroom level.

8   Copley, Freathy, and Walshe, *Teaching Biblical Narrative*, 14.

9   Leon McKenzie, *The Religious Education of Adults* (Birmingham: Religious Education Press, 1982), 116–28.

10 Copley, Freathy, and Walshe, *Teaching Biblical Narrative*, 8.

11 Walter Brueggemann, *Theology of the Old Testament: Testimony, Dispute, Advocacy* (Minneapolis: Fortress Press, 1997), 267.

12 Walter Brueggemann, *The Bible Makes Sense*, rev. ed. (Cincinnati: St. Anthony Messenger Press, 1989), 39.

13 Thomas Groome, *What Makes Us Catholic: Eight Gifts for Life* (San Francisco: HarperSanFrancisco, 2002), 135–67.

14 Margaret Nutting Ralph, *And God Said What? An Introduction to Biblical Literary Forms*, rev. ed. (New Jersey: Paulist Press, 2003), 4.

15 Richard Elliott Friedman, *Who Wrote the Bible?* (New York: HarperSanFrancisco, 1987), 15–32.

16 For a further discussion of the relationship between the Old and the New Testament, see Walter Brueggemann, *An Introduction to the Old Testament: The Canon and Christian Imagination* (Louisville: Westminster John Knox Press, 2003), 2–3.

17 St. Augustine. *"De sancta virginitate,"* 6:40, 399.

18 See Genesis 6:1-8. The Nephilim were legendary warriors who are described as the product of sons of God and daughters of men. This mythical reference is part of the pre-history that the biblical author uses to explain the corruption that had entered creation and motivated God to initiate a re-start with the great flood.

19 Thomas Groome, Keynote Address, When Faith Meets Pedagogy Conference: Toronto, October 2011.

20 Reginald Bibby, *Restless Gods: The Renaissance of Religion in Canada* (Ottawa: Novalis, 2004), 41–43. Bibby found that few Roman Catholics or mainline Protestants switch religious affiliation through marriage. It is much more likely to go the other way, where the religious minority switches due to the cultural sway of the majority.

21 While readers may wonder if Esau is really hungry or just really stupid, they should keep in mind that this story is part of a folkloric tradition that helps explain the later dominance of the Israelites (Jacob's ancestors) over the Edomites (Esau's ancestors).

22 Historical veracity is based on documentation and corroborating evidence. We do not have this kind of information and authentication with figures like Moses or King David or the youthful Jesus.

23 Our English word for *nabi* – "prophet" – is derived from the Greek word *pro-phates*, which means "one who speaks for another." See Lawrence Boadt, *Reading the Old Testament: An Introduction* (New York: Paulist Press, 1984), 306.

24 God's sacred name as revealed in the book of Exodus remains mysterious. Many scholars believe that YHWH is derived from the verb "to be" in Hebrew, which could lead to various translations: I am the one who is; I cause to be what I cause to be; I am the existent one; I will be with you. For a more detailed explanation see Bernhard W.

Anderson, *Understanding the Old Testament,* 4th ed. (New Jersey: Prentice-Hall, 1986), 62–63.

25 See the documentary film *With God on Our Side: George W. Bush and the Rise of the Religious Right.* Directed by Calvin Skaggs and David Van Taylor. 2004.

26 The first nine plagues can be organized in triplets, each with its own motif. At the same time, each triplet is organized with the same structure. For a more detailed explanation, see Boadt, *Reading the Old Testament,* 167–69.

27 Boadt, *Reading the Old Testament,* 169.

28 Boadt, *Reading the Old Testament,* 169.

29 American journalist Finley Peter Dunne first coined this expression in a Mr. Dooley article.

30 Elizabeth A. Johnson, *Truly Our Sister: A Theology of Mary in the Communion of Saints* (New York: Continuum, 2003), 195–99.

31 Raymond E. Brown, *101 Questions & Answers on the Bible* (New York: Paulist Press, 1990), 92–97.

32 "These three are called 'synoptic' because, in contrast to the Fourth Gospel (John), their presentation of Jesus can be seen (*-optic*) together (*syn-*). They can be arranged in three parallel columns, and different editions of such a synopsis have been published. Once they are viewed side by side in this way it becomes clear that Matthew, Mark and Luke describe the same basic events from the life of Jesus in roughly the same order and often with the exact same words. This suggests there is a literary relationship among those three Gospels, such that two of the authors have copied significant portions from one or two of the others." John L. McLaughlin, *The Questions of Jesus* (Ottawa: Novalis, 2001), 12–13.

33 John Dominic Crossan, *Jesus: A Revolutionary Biography* (San Francisco: HarperCollins, 1994), 83.

34 Boadt, *Reading the Old Testament,* 60.

35 For a further explanation of this common error, see Nutting Ralph, *And God Said What?* 211–18.

36 In the Old Testament, see 1 Kings 17 and 2 Kings 4:18-37. In the New Testament, see the following stories: Mark 5:21-24, 35-43; Luke 7:11-17; 8:40-56; and John 11.

37 Brueggemann, *The Bible Makes Sense*, 89–98.

38 Brueggemann, *The Bible Makes Sense*, 94.

39 John Shea, *Stories of God: An Unauthorized Biography* (Leominster, UK: Gracewing, 1989), 8.

40 See John 6:11. The celebration of Eucharist (giving thanks) comes from this passage in John's gospel.

41 In John's gospel, the evangelist connects the experience of manna in the desert to Jesus, who is the bread of life. See John 6:31-35.

42 Brueggemann, *The Bible Makes Sense*, 94. (Emphasis in original.)

43 Ronald Rolheiser, *The Holy Longing: The Search for a Christian Spirituality* (Toronto: Doubleday, 1999), 147.

44 Joan Chittister, *Songs of the Heart: Reflections on the Psalms* (Toronto: Novalis Publishing, 2011), 3.

45 Stephen Mitchell, *A Book of Psalms* (New York: HarperCollins Publishers, 1993), 4.

46 In addition to Joan Chittister's and Stephen Mitchell's works, here are two other excellent translations of the psalms: Nan. C. Merrill, *Psalms for Praying: An Invitation to Wholeness* (New York: Continuum, 2007); Christine Robinson, *Psalms for a New World* (http://doubterpsalms. blogspot.ca/).

47 For a fuller exploration of the distinction between law and gospel, I recommend Carl Walther's seminal work, *The Proper Distinction Between Law and Gospel* (St. Louis: Concordia, 1986).

48 See *The Catholic Youth Bible: New Revised Standard Version* (Winona, MN: St. Mary's Press, 2000).

Essential Books for Catholic Educators

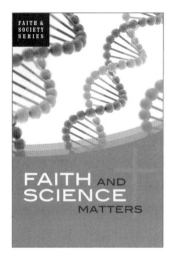

Faith and Science Matters
Series edited by Michael O'Hearn

Confronting misconceptions surrounding Catholic thought on various scientific developments, this collection of essays by leading scholars and educators helps us to understand Catholic teaching. Clear explanations offer us insights and ways to share the wealth of Church teaching on cosmology, creation, evolution, bioethics, ecology and technology.

144pp PB 978-2-89646-407-4 $18.95

The *Faith & Society Series* answers the burning questions of our time and shows Christianity's relevance to the many challenges of today's culture.

Building a Virtuous School:
Guided Reflections on Catholic Character Formation
By Ted Laxton

Using the framework of the theological, cardinal and communal virtues, Ted Laxton offers reflections on real-life school experiences and invites us to consider how we may build a truly Catholic culture in our schools. Each scenario and reflection guides us toward a common understanding of our mission and a shared sense of meaning, shaped and formed by the Catholic tradition.

144pp PB 978-2-89646-488-3 $18.95

NOVALIS
www.novalis.ca

Essential Books for Catholic Educators

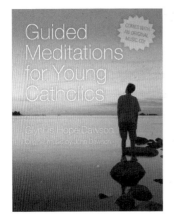

Guided Meditations for Young Catholics
By Glynnis Hope Dawson
Music by John Dawson

Introduce intermediate-aged youth to the richness of prayer and meditation, and help them discover the many varied ways of praying. Perfect for catechists and religious educators, this exceptional collection of prayers and meditations not only teaches youth how to pray, but also invites them to consider important themes of Christian faith, such as the gifts and fruits of the Holy Spirit, the liturgical seasons, social justice and forming authentic relationships with others.

Complementing this compilation of prayers is a CD of music by John Dawson, one of Canada's foremost liturgical composers. Youth will be drawn more deeply into the meditations and discover the grace that daily reflection offers us.

128pp PB with CD 978-2-89646-409-8 $29.95

Gifted by God: A Confirmation Retreat Kit
By David Dayler & Anne Jamieson

Religious educators will welcome this wonderful kit for creating a meaningful retreat for youth preparing for Confirmation. This retreat kit is an ideal companion to any sacramental preparation program, whether in the parish or school. It offers religious educators all the material — on a single DVD — needed for leading a retreat, including suggested schedules for full- and half-day retreats, leader's guide, prayer services, detailed activity plans, handouts and music.

DVD 978-2-89646-546-0 $39.95

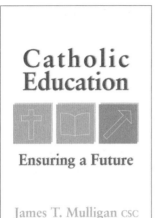

Catholic Education: Ensuring a Future
By James T. Mulligan, CSC

In *Catholic Education: Ensuring a Future*, Mulligan argues that everyone involved in Catholic education — parents and teachers, principals and superintendents, directors and trustees, priests and bishops — must own ever-greater responsibility and collaboration so that Catholic schools remain vibrant faith communities, offering students an authentic alternative to secular education.

336pp PB 978-2-89507-671-1 $24.95

High School Ministry from A to Z
By Brad Lewis

Written for new campus ministers as well as seasoned ones, *High School Ministry from A to Z* is filled with energy, ideas, inspiration and passion. School administration, clergy and high school staff — who are all integral parts of high school ministry — will discover how this important ministry can connect to their classroom, office and role within the school.

275pp PB 978-2-89646-036-6 $39.95

NOVALIS
www.novalis.ca

Essential Books for Catholic Educators

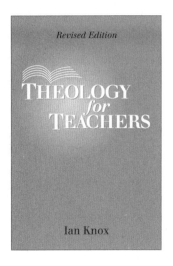

Theology for Teachers
By Ian Knox

This book is for anyone interested in a comprehensive and accessible introduction to the Catholic faith. It is ideal for those who are preparing to teach in Catholic schools, as it fills the need for a basic text suited to the curriculum guidelines of the Institute for Catholic Education for university courses in Catholic education.

384pp PB 978-2-89507-020-7 $29.95

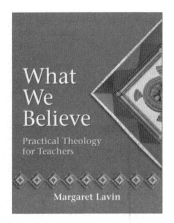

What We Believe: Practical Theology for Teachers
By Margaret Lavin

If teachers are going to teach their faith, they need to know what it is about. *What We Believe* outlines the major theological themes that ground our understanding of who we believe God is, and who we are in relationship to God. *What We Believe* is the essential theological guide for all religious educators.

174pp PB 978-2-89646-143-1 $24.95

Study Guide:
112pp PB 978-2-89646-144-8 $12.95

NOVALIS
www.novalis.ca